John Swan

Penguin Educatic

Penguin Moder
General Editor: B

Motivation an
Editors: Dalbir B

The Meanings of Fear
Stanley Rachman

Stanley Rachman

The Meanings of Fear

Penguin Education

Penguin Education
A Division of Penguin Books Ltd,
Harmondsworth, Middlesex, England
Penguin Books Inc, 7110 Ambassador Road,
Baltimore, Md 21207, USA
Penguin Books Australia Ltd,
Ringwood, Victoria, Australia
Penguin Books Canada Ltd,
41 Steelcase Road West,
Markham, Ontario, Canada

First published 1974

Made and printed in Great Britain by
C. Nicholls & Company Ltd,
The Philips Park Press, Manchester
Set in Times Roman

To Harry, Bern and both Lionels

Contents

Editorial Foreword 9

1 Introduction 11

2 'Fear is Not a Lump' 17

3 The Expression and Recognition of Fear 25

4 Reading our own Emotions 33

5 Innate and Early Fears 40

6 Types and Degrees of Fear 50

7 The Reduction of Fear 62

8 Interpretations: Traumatic Conditioning 76

9 Interpretations: Habituation and Sensitization 86

10 Interpretations: Psychoanalytic Views 92

11 Adaptive Fear 100

Appendix: Some Notes on Physiological Aspects of Fear 105

References 109

Index 113

Editorial Foreword

In *Meanings of Fear* Stanley Rachman tells the fascinating story of what modern psychology has found out about one of man's commonest emotions. He covers the whole range of phenomena from the simple apprehensions of everyday life to the acute phobias and paralysing anxieties seen in clinical cases. He describes what is known about the nature and causes of different fears and about the training methods that are proving effective in treating them. He presents hard evidence, some experimental, some clinical, to support his conclusions, and makes a point of saying what is still unknown and remains to be discovered by further research. And he does all this in remarkably clear and simple prose.

This volume arises naturally from Dr Rachman's background and experience in research and clinical practice. Trained as an experimental psychologist, he has contributed to the analysis of the environmental conditions and the internal bodily processes associated with fears. At the same time, working as a part of a team in the Maudsley Hospital, he has dealt with clinical cases and assessed the value of different types of treatment. The published works of Dr Rachman and his collaborators form an important part of modern psychology's knowledge about the theoretical and practical problems of neurotic disorders.

D.B. and J.S.

1 Introduction

This opening chapter delineates the scope of the book and introduces some of the main themes. In the first place, it is a discussion of *human* fears, their range, genesis, fluctuations and nature. Although little direct reference is made to the vast literature describing research into fear in animals, my conception of human fears has been considerably influenced by such research, particularly where it pertains to the induction and the avoidance of fear. Gray's recent interpretation, *The Psychology of Fear and Stress*, is an admirable guide to much of this research and has been a considerable help.

Although the word 'fear' is used without difficulty in everyday language to mean the experience of apprehension, problems arise when it is used as a scientific term. It cannot be assumed that people are always able, or even willing, to recognize and then describe the experience of fear. In wartime, admissions of fear are discouraged. Similarly, boys are usually discouraged from expressing fear. In surveys carried out on student populations, it has been found that the admission of certain fears by men is felt to be socially undesirable.

The social influences which obscure the accurate expression of fear further complicate the intrinsic difficulties involved in the recognition and description of our own experiences or predicted experiences. For instance, it is regularly found that there are numerous people who state on questionnaires that they are fearful of specific situations and are later seen to display fearless behaviour when placed in the specified situation. Subjective reports of fear also tend to be of limited value in assessing the intensity of the experience because of the difficulties involved in translating phrases such as 'extremely frightened', 'terrified', and 'slightly anxious' into a quantitative scale with stable properties.

For these reasons among others, psychologists have extended the study of fear beyond an exclusive reliance on subjective reports by including indices of physiological change and measures of overt behaviour. It is helpful to think of fear as comprising four main components: the subjective experience of apprehension, associated physiological changes, outward expressions of fear, and attempts to avoid or escape from certain situations. Altering a common saying, we might describe the experience as consisting of fear, flutter and flight.

When the four components of fear fail to correspond, as they commonly do, problems arise. People can experience subjective fear but remain outwardly calm and, if tested, show none of the expected psychophysiological reactions. We can also receive reports of subjective fear in the absence of any attempt at avoidance. The existence of these four components, coupled with the fact that they do not always correspond, makes it imperative in scientific exchanges to specify which component or aspect of fear one is referring to. Increasingly detailed studies of the phenomena of fear have naturally produced a more complex model, and it was with these considerations in mind that the title of this book was chosen.

In our everyday exchanges we rely for the most part on people *telling* us of their fears and then supplement this verbal information by interpreting their facial and other bodily expressions. Unfortunately, this kind of interpretation, when made in the absence of supporting contextual cues, can be misleading. Moreover, the value of observations of facial and related expressions is limited to certain categories of fear, particularly those of an acute and episodic nature. Diffuse and chronic fears are less visible. So we may observe signs of fear in an anxious passenger as an aircraft descends, but have few non-verbal cues of fear in a woman who is intensely apprehensive about ageing.

Although there are many types of fear, certain categories such as neurotic fears have understandably been studied more intensively than others. Among these varieties, a major division can be made between acute and chronic fears. The acute ones are generally provoked by tangible stimuli or situations and subside quite readily when the frightening stimulus is removed or avoided. The fear of snakes illustrates this acute type. A less common type of acute fear, seen sometimes in neurotic patients, is the sudden onset of panic which seems to have no tangible source. It can last for as long as an hour or more and often leaves a residue of discomfort. On the whole, the chronic fears tend to be more complex but, like the acute types, they may or may not be tied to tangible sources of provocation. The fear of being alone is an example of a chronic, tangible fear, but examples of chronic and intangible fears are by their very nature, difficult to specify. One simply feels persistently uneasy and anxious for unidentified reasons – a chronic state of dull aching fear which has been better described by novelists than by psychologists.

A distinction is sometimes drawn between fear and anxiety, where fear is taken to refer to feelings of apprehension about tangible and predominantly realistic dangers. Anxiety on the other hand is sometimes taken to refer to feelings of apprehension which are difficult to relate to tangible sources of stimulation. The inability to identify the source of the fear is usually regarded as the hallmark of anxiety and, in the case of psychodynamic theories, the inability is said to be a result of repression; hence the source of the fear remains unconscious. Although this distinction between fear and anxiety is not without its uses, it will not be retained for purposes of the present exposition. The division between tangible and intangible fears bears on another distinction which has proven to be *clinically* useful, that of focal versus diffuse fears. As we shall see, focal fears are more easily modified, despite the fact that they are often of longstanding duration.

Although it may be of little practical value, the distinction between innate and acquired fears is an intriguing one. The impact of early Behaviourism, with its massive emphasis on the importance of acquired behaviour, led to the interment of the notion that some fears may be innately determined. Even the possible existence of such fears in animals was only reluctantly conceded. For reasons to be discussed later, the possible occurrence of innately determined fears in human beings is once more under serious consideration.

The fluctuations of fears are of some interest, especially their emergence in early childhood followed by a general decline in frequency and intensity during middle to late childhood. The rise and fall of fears, as in childhood, raises questions of causation. What is the cause of fear? Or, more accurately, what are the causes of fears? The inevitable subsidiary question is, why do fears decline and disappear?

As an introduction, one can risk an oversimplified account of the major causes of fear. They include: exposure to a traumatic stimulation, repeated exposures to sub-traumatic (sensitizing) situations and observations (direct and indirect) of people exhibiting fear. Fears diminish as a result of repeated exposures to a mild or toned down version of the frightening situation – by a process akin to habituation. The decline in fears as a consequence of repetition can also be facilitated by superimposing on the fearful reactions an incompatible response (e.g.relaxation).

The complexity of the relations between the emergence and the decline of a fear can be seen from the fact that repeated exposures to the fear-evoking object or situation are said to sometimes increase the fear (sensitization) and at other times to decrease it (habituation). In other words, it is posited that fears exist in a state of balance. Furthermore, this balance will tilt in the direction of increased or decreased fear depending on the type of exposure, intensity of stimulation, the person's state of alertness and other factors.

The tendency to habituate to stimulation is a universal characteristic, but there are instances where habituation fails to occur. Some fear responses fall into this group of exceptions and are therefore considered to be abnormal in the restricted sense of undue persistence despite repeated exposures. They may be regarded as being abnormal in the clinical sense if the fearful reactions are also disproportionate and, to some extent, incapacitating.

There are of course wide individual variations in fearfulness and we now have some evidence of individual differences in the ease with which people habituate to stimulation. It is, of course, tempting to relate fearfulness to an inability to habituate satisfactorily and some interesting attempts have in fact been made.

Fear, or its first cousin, anxiety, plays a major part in most neurotic disorders. As a result, it is a subject which has greatly occupied clinicians and they and their research colleagues have explored the effects of a variety of therapeutic methods. Leaving aside the pharmacological methods which, although they are partly successful (Lader and Marks, 1971) fall outside the scope of this book, we are left with psychological methods for reducing fears. These can be divided into two main types: those which attempt directly to reduce the fear or anxiety (as in behaviour therapy) and those which attempt to modify the putative underlying causes of the fear or anxiety, as in psychoanalysis and related techniques.

The direct methods are comparatively new and largely the products of experimental psychology. The best established and most extensively used of the direct methods, desensitization, was recently joined by 'flooding' and by 'modelling'. Psychoanalysis is of course the most famous and influential of the indirect methods and has spawned many derivations. Most of them were, like psychoanalysis itself, developed by clinical psychiatrists or psychologists. The most widely practised form of indirect treatment is psychotherapy (a confusingly wide term covering many types of activity) and not psychoanalysis, which is, comparatively speaking, a rare form of therapy. Although there are great differences between techniques, the indirect methods share the assumption that a thorough exploration of matters seemingly unrelated to the pertinent fear, is a necessary prerequisite for the reduction of fear.

2 'Fear is Not a Lump'

Over the past twenty years, important advances have been made in our ability to reduce human fears. A great deal of the research was carried out on selected university students who exhibited strong but circumscribed fears (of snakes, spiders, public speaking and so on) and it was hoped that the findings would, by analogy, be applicable to other groups and other fears. In particular, it was hoped that a clearer understanding of pathological fears might emerge. The results are described in chapter 7, but the studies also produced some unexpected spin-off. In order to ensure that the experimental findings were reliable and replicable, it became necessary to develop instruments with which to measure degrees and types of fear.

The typical analogue fear study, carried out on a sample of female university students with mini-phobias, involved comparisons between treated and untreated groups of subjects. The effects of the experimental treatment were generally measured by a combination of instruments. It was found to be necessary to have a general questionnaire which could be applied to a large and unselected group of potential subjects in order to select those who report a substantial degree of fear of the object or situation in question. This initial selection is usually followed by another sorting test, usually called an 'avoidance test' or a 'behavioural approach test'. The subjects are assessed singly by asking them to approach as close as possible to the fearful object and, if they can, to handle it or simply touch it. During the conduct of this behavioural test, the subjects are asked to give a report of their subjectively experienced fear in terms of a 'fear thermometer', which is simply a scale of discomfort ranging from *calm* which is scored as zero, to *moderately fearful* which is scored at five, up to *terrified* which is scored at ten. The subjects are instructed in the use of the scale and are requested to use the full range. The subject's success or failure in the behavioural test is graded in some manner, usually in terms of her proximity to the feared object. This information is then combined with the subjective fear estimates provided on the fear thermometer. In a number of studies the behavioural and subjective measures have been supplemented by psychophysiological recordings, most typically those of cardiac rate, electrical resistance of the skin, muscle tension, respiration or some combination of these measures. In some instances the subject's behaviour during the behavioural tests has been rated on specific characteristics (e.g. tremors, pallor, etc.) by a group of external judges.

Although, as we shall see in later chapters, the various fear-reduction techniques have been shown to be impressively effective in general, some unexpected and complex findings have also emerged. Some perplexing occurrences have also been reported in the clinical application of these fear-reduction techniques. Despite the appearance of marked behavioural improvements, such as a claustrophobic patient acquiring the ability to travel on underground trains, patients sometimes deny that they have benefited from treatment. On other occasions the physiological reactions observed during the real or symbolic presentation of a fearful object diminish after treatment, but the patient may continue to complain of excessive fear.

Before it became clear that discrepancies between the various measures of fear are fairly common and even to be expected, a certain amount of confusion prevailed in therapeutic circles. Then it was also observed that among some patients the improvements apparent in their behaviour were followed only weeks or months later by subjective improvements as well. Repeated observations of this type led to the recognition that the different indices of fear might show different *rates* of response to treatment – a type of desynchrony. Recognition that the patient's subjective report tends to be the slowest to change brought some relief to therapists as well as patients. Roughly speaking, the order of change under therapeutic conditions is declining physiological reactivity, followed by behavioural improvements and, finally, by subjective improvements.

The poor correspondence between some measures of fear also led to difficulties in interpreting laboratory findings on fear-reduction. It even produced difficulties at the very earliest stage of experiments – the selection of suitably fearful subjects. It is a common experience to find that a substantial proportion of potential subjects who rate themselves as being fearful on a questionnaire will display only slight fear, or no fear at all, when exposed to the fearful object in a behavioural avoidance test. Some of them walk in, approach the snake directly and then lift it without hesitation in spite of having recorded on the questionnaire that they have an extreme fear of snakes. In laboratory research, as in clinical practice, it has been found that subjective reports of fear tend to diminish more slowly than overt signs of fear and avoidance behaviour.

An experimental example of a major discrepancy between different types of measure can be illustrated by the work of Paul (1966). In an analogue study on university students with a marked but circumscribed fear of public speaking, he assessed fear by a number of self-report measures, two major physiological measures, external ratings of fear and a behavioural test of public speaking. The outcome of the experiment was therapeutically successful and a good deal of useful subsidiary information was gathered. Paul found a reasonably high correlation between all the self-report measures of therapeutic improvement, but there was little relationship between the physiological indicants of fear and there was no relation between the self-report indices and the physiological ones (pp. 61–4). There was a modest correlation between the therapist's and the subject's ratings of improvement (p. 64). It is interesting to notice that, despite this lack of agreement between some of the outcome measures, all the major ones (including self-report and physiological indices) showed that the treated subjects were significantly improved both at termination of treatment and at follow-up.

Peter Lang of Wisconsin University, who has been responsible for some of the most valuable research and theorizing on the subject of fear and fear reduction, expressed the new view of fear extremely well: '. . . fear is not some hard phenomenal lump that lives inside people, that we may palpate more or less successfully' (Lang, 1970). He has argued convincingly that fear responses are related to each other, but only in an imperfect manner; they are partially independent. In many circumstances, however, they do show corresponding changes. In one of Lang's experiments, a correlation of 0·41 between the subject's rating of fear and his avoidance behaviour was obtained. Again, there was a correlation of 0·48 between the subject's report of fear in the test situation and the estimate made by an external observer. On the other hand, in the same experiment he found a correlation of only 0·04 between questionnaire data and overtly expressed fear in the avoidance test.

In a study on automated desensitization (Lang, Melamed and Hart, 1970), a reassuringly high correspondence between fear reports and heart rate was obtained. Respiratory rate, however, showed a disappointingly low correlation with subjective fear; only 0·05. To paraphrase some of Lang's writings, fear comprises a set of imperfectly coupled systems.

Without doing too much injustice to the finer points of this extensive research, the present position can be summarized like this. Self-reports of fear correlate well with each other; they correlate moderately well with the ratings of fear made by external judges and also with the avoidance behaviour observed in a fear test, particularly when the avoidance behaviour and self-reports are graded in a few large steps; self-reports correlate modestly with physiological indices of fear; physiological indices of fear correlate modestly with each other and hardly at all with muscle tension.

Another point worth mentioning is the strong likelihood that *all* correlations between the various measures or response systems are likely to increase at extremes of the scales. In other words, the correspondence between the different measures will be greater in conditions of extreme fear or extreme calmness. To take the simple case, in a state of deep relaxation it is likely that the self-report of subjects will be one of calmness, the physiological response systems will be relatively quiescent, there will be no avoidance behaviour and an external observer would describe the state as being one of calmness. The belief that, at extreme levels of fear a high degree of correspondence between measures will be obtained, is based partly on clinical anecdote and partly on some scattered research findings.

In an investigation of fear among parachute jumpers, Fenz and Epstein (1967) found evidence of both correspondence and lack of correspondence between different measures. In a group of ten veteran jumpers, discordant results were obtained. The three physiological measures all showed a steady increase during the entire jumping sequence. This was contrary to the pattern observed in the measure of subjective fear which varied in the following way – increase in fear, then decrease, followed once more by an increase (see Figure 1 overleaf). Among the group of ten novices however, subjective fear and psychophysiological reactions showed corresponding patterns of increase and decrease. Heart rate, skin conductance and respiration all built up to a peak (e.g. the heart-rate mean equalled 145 beats per minute) shortly before the jump occurred and then subsided again fairly quickly after landing. The veterans experienced only mild increases in heart rate, subjective fear and other measures, where the novices displayed extremely strong reactions. These findings support the idea that the correspondence between measures will be seen to increase at extreme levels of fear or, at the opposite extreme, calmness.

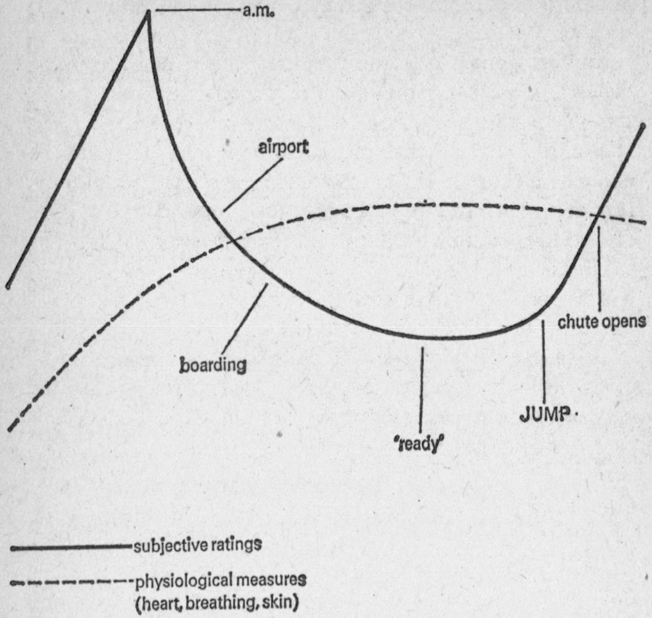

Figure 1 The discordant results obtained in a study of fear in veteran parachute jumpers. Their subjective fear reports do not correspond to the changes in physiological activity. Adapted from Fenz and Epstein (1967) and Epstein and Fenz (1965)

In view of the imperfect coupling between systems, what is the best basis for predicting the occurrence of fear? Following the advice of Lang and others, it might be best to avoid reliance on a single measure. Self-report of experienced fear seems to be indispensable and, at the same time, potentially misleading. It would appear from the work of Griffiths and Joy (1971) among others, that self-report data can provide a useful if crude basis for prediction of fear and have some practical advantages over more elaborate techniques of assessment. Providing one does not ask too much of a self-report measure, in the sense of too great a degree of refinement, it can be valuable. The inclusion of a behavioural approach test is highly desirable in almost all circumstances and it will of course provide a valuable check on the predictive value of a self-report measure. The ratings of fear made by external judges can be useful but, as we shall see in the next chapter, they are not free of problems. Some physiological indices, and in particular heart rate, can provide useful data for prediction purposes. It has, for example, been shown that heart rate acceleration is frequently correlated with the imaginal rehearsal of fear situations (e.g. Lang, Melamed and Hart, 1970; Mathews, 1971). Measures of skin conductance have sometimes been shown to have some value, but there are large individual differences in responsiveness and the index produces technical problems arising out of its rapid adaptation. Practically no success has been achieved with measures of muscular tension.

Some of the dangers of incautious use of a single measure include the following. Too great a reliance on self-report can lead one to underestimate a person's degree of courage; too great a reliance on approach behaviour observed in a fear test can lead one to underestimate the degree of a person's *fear*.

If one pursues this new view of fear as a complex of imperfectly coupled response systems, it leads to some amusing new ideas on the nature of courage. As we have seen, a person may be quite willing to approach a frightening object or situation but experience a high degree of subjective fear and even some unpleasant bodily accompaniments. This persistence in the face of subjective and bodily feelings of fear comes closest to the common-sense view of courage – to continue despite one's fear. A psychologist could describe this type of courageous behaviour as an example of uncoupling, in which the person's overt behaviour advances beyond his subjective discomfort.

Is a person who continues to approach a fearful situation in the absence of any subjective fear or bodily accompaniments, to be described as courageous or not? Presumably, in psychological parlance, he would have to be described as someone who displays an absence of fear rather than the presence of courage. We also have to consider how we would regard a person who feels subjectively calm when approaching a fearful situation but, on measurement displays clear physiological disturbances? An autonomic coward? Contrariwise, a person who shows no physiological disturbances when experiencing subjective fear can be said to possess a brave autonomic system.

Perhaps we should reserve the description of 'true courage' for those people who are willing and able to approach a fearful situation, despite the presence of subjective fear, psychophysiological disturbances and intense bodily reactions. It will be evident that our expanding conception of fear has provoked some entertaining ideas and that there are many more yet to come.

3 The Expression and Recognition of Fear

Do our bodies, and especially our faces, convey accurate information about our emotional feelings and, in particular, the experience of fear? If fear *is* manifest in our physical appearance, can other people 'read' us correctly? Can other people recognize when we are frightened even if we refrain from telling them? And on the other side, can we gauge when other people are fearful, even if they refrain from informing us of their feelings? Is fear expressed in the same manner by people living in different parts of the world?

Darwin was one of the first scientists to tackle these questions and his views are still of considerable interest. In *The Expressions of the Emotions*, he argued that although most forms of emotional expression are 'innate' or inherited and cannot be said to depend on the will of the individual, those actions which are followed by satisfactory events will become habitual. One of his 'principles of expression' has a surprisingly modern flavour for psychologists: 'The first of these principles is that movements which are serviceable in gratifying some desire, or in relieving some sensation, if often repeated, become so habitual that they are performed, whether or not of any service, whenever the same desire or sensation is felt, even in a very weak degree' (p. 348).

Darwin was one of the first people to give a systematic account of the gradation from 'mere attention to a start of surprise', turning into fear and finally, 'into extreme terror and horror'. Although some of his descriptions of the gestures supposedly expressive of emotion are extravagant and occasionally border on the comical, his account of the characteristic manifestations of fear is vivid and largely in keeping with modern accounts:

The frightened man first stands like a statue motionless and breathless . . . the heart beats quickly and violently . . . the skin instantly becomes pale . . . perspiration immediately exudes from the skin and as the surface is then cold, (we have what is termed) a cold sweat . . . the hairs also on the skin stand erect and the superficial muscles shiver . . . in connection with the disturbed action of the heart, the breathing is hurried . . . the mouth becomes dry . . . one of the best marked symptoms is the trembling of all of the muscles of the body and this is often first seen in the lips.

Later in the same chapter (12) Darwin described the transition from fear into terror:

The heart beats wildly or may fail to act and faintness ensue; there is a death-like pallor; the breathing is laboured; the wings of the nostrils are widely dilated . . . there is a gulping of the throat, protruding eyeballs, dilated pupils, rigid muscles. (In the final stages) as fear rises to an extreme pitch, the dreadful scream of terror is heard. Great beads of sweat stand on the skin. All the muscles of the body are relaxed. Utter prostration soon follows, and the mental powers fail. The intestines are affected. The sphincter muscles cease to act, and no longer retain the contents of the body.

Although Darwin's beliefs about the extent to which the facial expression of emotions (such as fear) are universal to all mankind have received only partial support, he seems seldom to have gone badly wrong. Furthermore, some of the types of evidence and means of collection used by him (e.g. judgements of pictorially displayed emotions, cross-cultural comparisons, etc.) are still in use today.

No one would quarrel with his views that both nature and nurture contribute to the expression of emotions; in fact only small advances have been made since Darwin's day and these mainly in the analysis of facial displays of emotion. On the question of universal forms of emotional display, which Darwin believed to exist, there has been a slight increase in knowledge. As we shall see, some types of expression are probably universal (e.g. in happiness) while others, as in fear, appear to be somewhat confined culturally. Incidentally, Darwin was especially astute in acknowledging that an emotional display may occur universally but not be recognized universally. To take a hypothetical example: if joy were universally expressed by a twitch of the left ear, it would not necessarily follow that everyone would recognize either the twitch or its meaning.

For a period, particularly in the 1920s, experimental psychologists devoted a great deal of attention to these questions. One of the most prominent investigators, Professor Landis, carried out some extraordinary experiments and the conclusions which he drew from these studies were discouraging. This well-known research, later supported by the work of Sherman, led to pessimistic conclusions and more or less closed this chapter in experimental psychology. During the past decade, however, the vigorous attempts of Ekman, Friesen and Ellsworth (1972) to revive interest in the non-verbal expression and recognition of emotions have helped to prise open the door once more.

The pessimists, led by Landis and Sherman, concluded that we cannot accurately identify someone else's emotions, including that of fear. It was argued that our occasional successes in identification were largely the result of our knowledge of the circumstances which had led up to the behaviour under observation. Without excavating the detailed findings of this research, it is still worthwhile considering the *type* of experimental evidence on which their conclusions were founded. In his most remarkable experiment, Landis took a large number of photographs of the facial expression of the twenty-five volunteers who were subjected to each of seventeen provoking experiences. Until this time most psychologists had relied on the posed facial expressions of actors as their test material and, in order to overcome the objections to this artificiality, Landis attempted to obtain material derived from genuine and spontaneous expressions of emotion. He went to great lengths and his subjects were exposed to some extremely unpleasant situations, including one or two of dubious character. The subjects were deceived into taking a breath of ammonia, given an electric shock without warning and, most extraordinary of all, required to decapitate a live rat.

Examination of the results showed that there were no facial expressions characteristic of any of the situations and there were no expressions which were consistently correlated with the subject's verbal report of how he felt at the time. Furthermore, external judges were unable to identify the significance of the expressions with any accuracy or guess what the provoking circumstances might have been. In all, Landis argued that facial expressions convey little useful information about emotional states. So in the case of fear, for example, he argued that one cannot tell from a person's facial expression whether he is frightened or not.

Landis was persuasive and it was only after contrary findings had been reported on a number of occasions in later years that his own experimental methods were subjected to closer scrutiny and for a number of reasons found to be unsatisfactory. As the subjects were passed from one provoking situation to the next without much delay, it is highly probable that Landis was photographing the consequences of a cumulative disturbance rather than the response to seventeen discrete provocations. It has also been pointed out that the provoking situations are unlikely to have elicited the same emotion in all of his subjects and there is internal evidence that the men and women, for example, were responding differently. It is also clear from internal evidence that many of the experimental conditions failed to elicit any emotional reaction whatever. For these and a number of other reasons, it is not entirely surprising that Landis was unable to obtain clear evidence of characteristic forms of emotional expression in the faces of his subjects.

The views of Landis received substantial support from the findings reported by Sherman to the effect that nurses, psychologists and medical students had little success in identifying the emotional reactions of very young infants. The observers were shown a series of babies immediately after they had been stimulated by each of four types of stimulus which were intended to evoke the reactions of hunger (missing a feeding period), fear (being dropped), anger (being restrained) and pain (being pricked). Some of the observers were shown filmed recordings of the babies reactions, while others observed them *in vivo.* In neither condition were the observers successful in identifying the hypothetical emotions. However, when the stimuli causing the reactions of the infants were also shown to observers, the degree of success in identifying the various emotions was far greater. In the case of fear, for example, the success rate increased from 20 per cent without the antecedent information, to as high as 70 per cent when the infants were seen to be dropped. Rather more importance was attached to these findings than might have been justified. At the most, his conclusion should have been restricted to the expression and recognition of emotional behaviour in very young infants – they were in fact less than eight days old and it is more than likely that differentiation of emotional reactions does not emerge clearly until a much later stage of development. Later research by Goodenough, carried out on a one-year-old infant, produced a much higher success rate in the recognition of emotional reaction. Although the sixty-eight observers were correct in judging astonishment in 94 per cent of their attempts, their assessment of fear produced a disappointingly low figure of 21 per cent correct.

The methods of examining problems related to the expression of fear continue to rely to a large extent on the judgements made by selected observers of the emotions which are presumed to be portrayed, either spontaneously or artificially, in still photographs, motion films and video-tapes. However, in order to assemble the judgements of the observers, it is necessary to classify them in some manner, and this has led to the construction of *categories* of emotion. Most of the schemes extend to between four and seven classes and they generally include happiness, sadness, anger, disgust, fear and surprise. These last two categories – fear and surprise – often prove to be inseparable. In passing, it is a little cheering to note that the most easily distinguished and recognized of all forms of emotional expression is *happiness.*

Another way of classifying observed emotions is to use *dimensions* rather than categories and here the most useful scales appear to be, pleasant–unpleasant and passive–active.

In this sort of dimensional scheme, fear tends to lie towards the unpleasant and active ends of the dimensions. The classification of judgements of emotional reaction has been used in research into the behaviour of blind and sighted children. In the best known of these studies, the observers had a fair degree of success but in all instances the fears portrayed by the blind children were less accurately recognized than those of the sighted children. In both groups of children, the observers were better able to recognize 'happiness' and 'sadness' than 'fear'. These findings, taken in conjunction with those from cultural comparisons mentioned below, suggest that the non-verbal expression of fear is determined by both innate and acquired factors, with the latter predominating. On the other hand, the non-verbal expression of happiness seems to be determined more by innate factors than by acquired ones. We might expect, therefore, that a Chinese baby brought up in Leeds would show happiness in a similar way to his cousin reared in Chungking, but they may well display fear in dissimilar ways.

On the question of whether or not there are universal forms of emotional expression, Darwin's views are still serviceable and current assessments tend in the direction of recognizing limited instances of universality. In plain language, a few types of emotional expression seem to be common to all cultures. In the nature of the matter, a conclusive statement will never be possible because of the insuperable practical and technical problems involved; nevertheless, some small measure of agreement in both emotional expression and recognition is reported from cultures as diverse as the United States and remote areas of Borneo. The greatest agreement is generally found in the recognition of 'happiness' and, as before, 'fear' and 'surprise' cannot be disentangled. 'Fear' is sometimes confused with either 'anger' and/or 'disgust'. The findings from cross-cultural studies show interesting similarities to those reported on blind children and, in general, support the view that the non-verbal expression of fear is largely a matter of learning.

Attempts have also been made to specify which *components* of facial expression are involved in specific emotions but little progress has been made, perhaps because it is premature to go into details before the broader forms of expression are better understood. We are not in a position to say that particular muscle movements are involved in the expression of say, 'disgust' and yet others involved in the expression of 'anger', but we are within sight of means by which we may detect small component differences in the expression of pleasant and unpleasant emotions. It is of course recognized that the eyes are important in the expression of fear (and sadness) while the mouth is important in signifying happiness, anger or disgust.

As we have seen, a good deal of effort has gone into attempts to isolate the crucial, *non-verbal* expressions of fear and other emotions. In practice, however, the expression of fear is rarely restricted to non-verbal communication. Moreover, the display almost inevitably occurs in an understandable context and this greatly assists in the identification of the emotion which is being experienced. All of this means that in everyday life we are faced with a far easier task than that of the experimental observers. Consequently we should, and probably do, make fewer errors of judgement.

At the risk of oversimplifying a lot of research data, it seems that we are more likely to recognize general categories rather than specific types of emotional expression, assess happiness more accurately than fear or surprise, interpret better in context and make fewer errors when a person responds verbally as well as physically. Errors of judgement are greater where fear is concerned, where people from greatly differing backgrounds are involved, in the very young or in the silent.

Judgements made out of context will have a higher error

rate. Errors of judgement also arise as a result of deceptions – the 'actor' may control his overt reactions or transform them (e.g. feign sadness rather than display happiness). It is often assumed that people devote a lot of effort to disguising their emotional experiences – a process which is aptly called *denial.* There is no doubt at all that, at times, we all prefer not to convey our emotional feelings. Indeed the absence of such restraints would result in chaos. It may be however, that the frequency and importance of the phenomenon of denial has been exaggerated. An extension of the concept of denial to include emotional feelings of which we are not conscious, as in psychoanalytic theories, raises a nice philosophical point.

Those occasions (and there are many of them) on which we experience subjective feelings of fear but nevertheless display fearless approach behaviour are exceedingly interesting but they are not examples of what is meant by the technical term denial. However, it is proper that, having discussed the recognition of other people's emotions, we should now turn to a consideration of how successful we are at recognizing our own.

4 Reading our own Emotions

The psychological approach to the question of reading our own emotions has centred predominantly on the recognition and interpretation of internal bodily states. We are easily able to distinguish between approach and avoidance behaviour and this gross distinction is of little interest. Facial and other external manifestations of expressive behaviour are less readily available and even those which are, such as trembling and perspiring, have played little part in this type of investigation. However, the recognition and interpretation of internal bodily changes has been a subject of major concern almost since the emergence of modern psychology. In 1890, William James proposed a revolutionary theory of emotion which stated that our recognition of these bodily changes is the emotion itself. An over-simplified but nevertheless telling example of the application of the theory is that 'we feel frightened because we are running away'. According to James, 'common sense says we lose our fortune, are sorry and weep; we meet a bear, are frightened and run; we are insulted by a rival, are angry and strike ... but the more rational statement is that we feel sorry because we cry.'

In support of his theory, James argued that when they played emotional scenes, actors experienced the relevant emotional feeling. He also said that it is impossible to have an emotional reaction without the accompanying bodily sensations such as palpitations, dryness of the mouth, and so on.

This highly original theory is contradicted by several types of evidence and argument and has few supporters. The most pertinent objections for our purposes are these. Despite many intensive and sophisticated attempts to link specific bodily states and reactions with subjective emotional report, the results have been almost entirely unsuccessful. With some slight exceptions, it has proved impossible to either detect or deduce a person's emotional state from a study of his bodily or physiological reactions. Instead, one finds only a broad division between differing levels of arousal or activation of the system – certainly far too crude a division to lend credibility to James's theory that we experience the emotion by recognizing internal bodily changes. Closely related to this objection is the fact that the organs and systems which mediate the bodily changes which James was discussing are relatively insensitive and only slow to react – again, an inadequate source for the rapid and complex range of subjective emotional feelings. Lastly, it was discovered that the direct and artificial stimulation (e.g. by drugs) of the organs and systems responsible for mediating the bodily changes involved did not produce the expected emotional reactions. The drug which was used in most of these experiments, adrenaline, is capable of producing widespread and intense activation of the sympathetic nervous system, and the subjects who were given administrations of the drug did in fact display the normal physiological reactions, such as increased heart rate, sweating, increased respiration and so on. What they did not experience, however, was a normal and genuine emotional reaction. Instead they described what finally became called the 'as if' reaction. Subjects would characteristically describe an unusual experience in which they felt 'as if' something were about to happen, but only rarely did they give accounts of experiences that corresponded with their idea of previous emotional experiences and the majority of them were able to distinguish between the drug-induced reactions and a genuine emotional state. In the case of this theory at least, uncommon sense did not succeed.

A theory which comes closer to the common-sense view was proposed by Cannon, who recognized that the experience of emotion and the associated bodily feelings may occur in association or independently. Cannon's theory placed undue reliance on one particular structure of the brain, the hypothalamus, but the emphasis on cognitive factors in emotional experience, and acknowledgement that emotional (internal) reactions and subjective feelings may run independent courses, were both useful advances. A modern version of this theory which places even greater emphasis on the person's cognitive appraisal of the situation was proposed by Schachter and his colleagues. Starting from the fact that the range and subtlety of subjective emotional feelings far exceeds the restricted number of bodily (visceral) reactions, they argued that the way in which we view the situation 'exerts a steering function'. When bodily feelings are aroused, it is our appreciation of the situation in which we find ourself that determines 'whether the state of physiological arousal will be labelled as "anger", "joy", "fear", or whatever.' Contrary to the view put forward by James, they argue that 'the state of physiological arousal alone is not sufficient to induce an emotion'.

Schachter put forward some novel propositions and illustrated them in a number of interesting experiments. In the first place, even if the person finds himself in a situation of great danger but remains without accompanying bodily sensations (such as trembling, etc.), he will not experience fear. If, on the other hand, in that same situation of danger he has bodily reactions which are appropriate, he will then experience genuine fear. Lastly, if those same bodily reactions are experienced in a pleasant and festive situation, they will be labelled by the person as 'happiness' or 'joy'. Evidence in support of this view of emotional behaviour was obtained in a number of experiments during which subjects were given injections of adrenaline or an inert substance and then placed in a specially contrived situation with an experimental stooge who displayed either euphoric or angry behaviour. Schachter and Singer interpreted their results as showing that, given the bodily reactions produced by the drug, their experimental subjects reported that they felt either euphoric or angry depending on which type of behaviour the provoking stooge had displayed. In those subjects among whom no bodily reactions were stimulated (because an inert substance was used), there was little evidence of their having experienced either of these two emotional states, i.e. anger or euphoria. Taken at face value, the interpretation of the experiments supports the hypothesis that emotional feelings are far less likely to be experienced in the absence of aroused bodily states, but that once bodily states *are* aroused, we tend to interpret the ensuing emotion in terms of the situation in which we find ourselves.

If, as seems to be the case, it is possible to distinguish between high and low levels of these bodily states (or levels of arousal), then it seems possible that our cognitive appraisal of the situation will indeed 'exert a steering function'. Unfortunately the ingenuity of much of Schachter's work is not always matched by the experimental rigour one would like to see and it might be best to regard the findings as tentative. Some of the technical difficulties involved in the interpretation of these studies include the failure to ascertain their subjects' understanding of the situation in which they found themselves; determinations of the bodily states appear to have been taken before and after rather than during the subject's exposure to the stooge situation; in both of the experiments there were some subjects who behaved contrary to theoretical predictions and so on. While bearing these reservations in mind, the notion that when in a state of physiological arousal, people can quite readily be manipulated into feeling either euphoric or angry or, presumably, fearful, is an intriguing one.

One of Schachter's main propositions, that an emotional experience will not occur in the absence of physiological arousal, would appear to be contradicted by some of the facts alluded to in chapter 2. It will be recalled that discordances between subjective emotional feeling and bodily reaction have been repeatedly observed. For example, veteran parachutists report little subjective fear despite the presence of quite marked physiological reactivity. In another context, phobic subjects will sometimes report high levels of fear but display no physiological disturbance. These observations imply a need to revise Schachter's proposals and the resulting modifications may simplify matters.

A poorly developed skill

Returning to the specific question of whether or not we are capable of recognizing or 'reading' our internal emotional reactions, and particularly those associated with fear, it must be admitted that we do not seem to be talented. Subjects whose internal reactions are being electronically monitored can give accurate reports of these inner reactions at extreme levels of high or low arousal, but their estimates made in the extensive middle-ground between the two extremes are poor. For example, most people can assess the state of tension in their major muscle groups when they are in a flaccid or tight condition. However, it is commonly observed that they will report feeling relaxed even when these major muscles are in a state of tension. Contrariwise, they often describe localized muscle tension despite an absence of recorded flexion. Heart rate can be estimated best when it is sharply accelerated but, under other conditions, our guesses are poor. Another useful index of internal arousal, the electrical resistance of the skin, is of course unknown to most people and even instruction in its meaning and significance would not make its fluctuations accessible.

The signs on which we rely in attempting to gauge our own reactions consist mainly of heart palpitations, tremor, muscle tension, stomach discomfort, respiratory disturbance, sweating and dryness of the mouth. As in the case of heart rate, these signs seem to reach recognition threshold only at extreme levels. We are not able to pick up the smaller changes in muscle tension, or sweating, or even of tremor. In sum, we can only read the headlines.

It is probable that there are large individual differences in the ability to read one's own reactions but the range of variation and its relation to other individual attributes is unknown. An even more interesting question is whether or not we can learn to improve our internal reading ability. For reasons to be given, it seems certain that we can.

Apart from the intrinsic pleasure which improved reading would provide ('know thyself' in modern dress?), it may well lead the way to practical benefits. The most obvious application would lie in the direction of improved self-regulation of emotional reactions and expression. Early and accurate recognition of the premonitory signs of fear – or anger – may enable one to engage in more effective alternate and adaptive behaviour.

The major reason for confidently expecting that we can learn to improve our internal reading rests on exciting recent advances in the learned control of our internal processes and reactions. Although Russian psychologists have for some years now claimed that they are able to condition some surprising changes in internal processes (e.g. kidney functions), the immediate impetus for Western research came from Skinner's important work on operant conditioning and Neal Miller's brilliant research on the conditioning of autonomic nervous system functions in small animals. Leaving aside the considerable theoretical problems of Skinner's general 'system', the practical and technological advances which it produced have now been applied to the control of heart rate, skin resistance and even to changes in the electrical activity of the brain.

The principal method used in regulating these functions is called feedback control. It has repeatedly been shown that if you provide people with clear information about the particular function in question (e.g. heart rate) and instruct them to increase or decrease the rate, they can usually manage to do so within a few practice sessions. There are of course limits to the degree of control which it is possible to achieve and it has been found that continuous monitoring and rewards are desirable for good results. To date, most of these reports claim limited and short-term increases in the control of inner functions; enduring control may be far more difficult to obtain. Nonetheless the major step has now been taken and this achievement of conscious control of inner functions pertinent to emotion, encourages the hope that we can now learn to improve our reading.

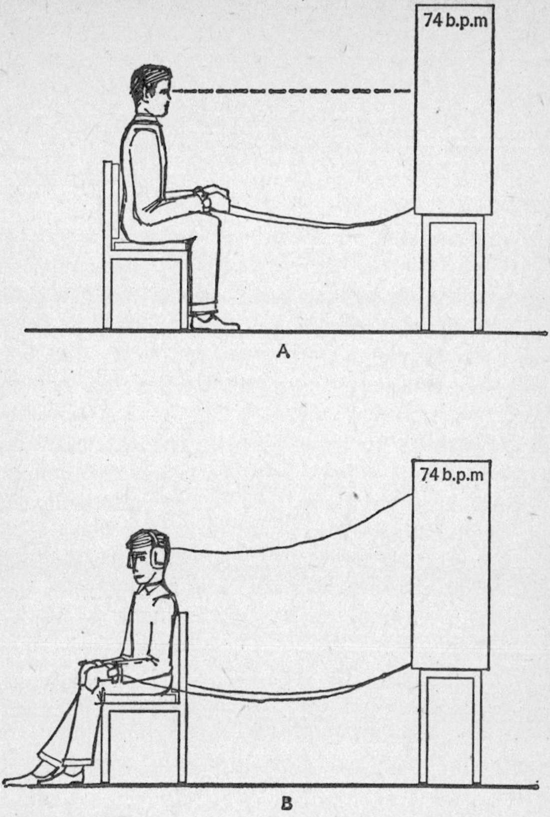

Figure 2 Acquiring control of cardiac activity. These two sketches illustrate simple laboratory arrangements for training subjects to acquire control. In the first (A), the subject's cardiac rate is fed into a visual display and he is instructed to increase or decrease his 'score'. In the second (B) his cardiac rate is transformed into an auditory signal which informs him of increases and decreases. Limited short-term changes can be obtained easily but substantial and/or enduring changes are more difficult to achieve

5 Innate and Early Fears

Dissatisfaction with introspectionist psychology led to the development of Behaviourism early in this century. Although it was primarily a revolution in methodology, Behaviourism also introduced new borders for psychology. The early growth of this new psychology was shaped by an understandable but unnecessary fusion of Behaviourism with Environmentalism – the view that most or all important aspects of human behaviour are explicable in terms of nurture rather than nature. There is no necessary connection between these ideas and 'neo-behaviourists', who are simply experimentalists with a special interest in the psychology of learning who have successfully separated environmentalism from a behaviouristic methodology (e.g. Hebb, Eysenck, Gray, Miller). As a result, the interesting relations between nature and nurture can be considered as problems in their own right.

Deciding whether some form of behaviour is innate or not is no easy matter, especially where people are concerned. For the most part, as in considering human *fears*, we are forced to resort to argument by exclusion. If we encounter fear which is seemingly impossible to account for in terms of the person's past experiences, we may then raise the subject of innate determinants. The absence of appropriate learning experiences is still the main basis for deciding whether fears are innate or acquired. Regrettably, this criterion was associated with a number of unnecessary assumptions which have confused discussions of innate fears. Three of the major nuisances are worth noting in order to discard them.

It was assumed that innate fears are (or should be)

immutable, common to all members of a species and *present* at all times and all ages. It is now obvious how these three assumptions precluded any possibility of recognizing innate fears. For one thing, we are aware that fears fluctuate and that they are age-related. These facts tell us nothing about how the fears are generated; they could as easily be innate or learned. Moreover, innate fears can appear in childhood by a process resembling maturation (see below).

We have also learned how to modify fears, innate or not. In animal studies, the modification of innate behaviour, including fears, is readily demonstrated. In recent years however, several writers have again postulated the existence of some innate fears in *people* (e.g. fear of the dark, snakes, strangers). It is difficult to confirm or deny these claims. Despite some suggestive evidence, such as the sharply skewed frequency distribution (i.e. unusually common occurrence) of certain fears such as that of snakes, it remains an open question.

There are less grounds for hesitation about acknowledging the existence of innate fears in animals. Some of the examples of innate fears in animals mentioned by Gray (1971) include 'mobbing' in chaffinches and a fear of snakes in many chimpanzees. Marks (1969) has also drawn attention to the evidence of innate fears among monkeys. Most impressive are the observations on isolated monkeys who were exposed to selected slides of other monkeys in threatening, fearful, playful and other poses. Sackett (1966) found that pictures illustrating threatening monkeys elicited fearful behaviour in the isolates and hence concluded that he was tapping an 'innate releasing mechanism'. Furthermore, the fearful reactions emerged in the third month of life and therefore provide an excellent example of the maturation of an innate fear. The reactions were observed to wane by the sixth month; possibly an illustration of the process of habituation of fear.

Although one cannot be certain that it is an innate pattern, human infants begin to evidence fear of strangers between six and eight months of age (sometimes called 'eight-month anxiety') after showing indiscriminate smiling responses in the earlier months. Marks has also raised the possibility that a fear of being stared at may be innate, quoting evidence of such a fear among monkeys. While the presence of this fear is evident in many socially anxious people (i.e. gaze avoidance), the animal evidence falls short of providing sufficient grounds for considering it to be innate in *humans.* Marks proposes other examples of innate fears, such as the fear of a visual cliff and other perceptual stimuli.

Sudden, novel or intense

However, as human infants exhibit fear in response to a wide range of sudden, novel or intense stimuli, it may be preferable to determine which stimulus attributes are innately capable of evoking fear. Another important question which will be discussed later is whether we can ascertain individual differences in susceptibility to acquire fears and, if so, is this susceptibility innate?

Gray (1971) has formulated a useful and simple guide: '... it would appear to be possible to subsume all fear stimuli under one of four general principles: intensity, novelty, "special evolutionary dangers" ... and stimuli arising from social interaction' (p. 20). Although it might be possible to collapse the attribute of suddenness into a combination of intensity and novelty, there are grounds for adding it to Gray's list of four principles. He also discusses another type of fear-eliciting situation which is described as a 'lack of stimulation'. He quotes as an example the failure of a stimulus to occur 'at a point in time or space where it usually occurs' and this may act like a novel stimulus. Moving on to a much more complex level of analysis, one wonders whether this absence of expected and familiar stimulation may play a part in the commonly seen clinical condition known as separation anxiety. It may also provide the basis for an explanation of the extremely common fear of darkness.

Gray points out that stimuli which are classed under the principles of intensity or novelty (e.g. noise, strange objects, pain, etc.) tend to diminish readily with age. In other terms, they are subject to habituation. He contrasts these types of stimuli with the special fears of 'predators and conspecifics', which take time to mature. This group of fears – in humans they would be classified under the heading of 'social interactions' – show a gradual *increase* with age. As we shall see, there is evidence to demonstrate a crossover in the sources in most of our fears and this occurs roughly at the end of childhood and beginning of adolescence.

The gradual decline in fears associated with intense and novel stimulation smacks of habituation, whereas the increase in social fears suggests a process of increasing sensitization. One must bear in mind that there are exceptions however, as we have seen in the case of the fear of strangers which emerges at roughly six months but wanes at the end of the child's first year. Presumably social fears are also subject to a form of habituation and will be observed at a molar level as an increase in social confidence. Returning to the fears which appear to be based on sudden, intense or novel stimulation, Gray provides a succinct statement: 'It seems that we come into the world ready to be frightened by any intense or novel stimuli, but readily become used to such stimuli, provided that they are not followed by any more disastrous consequences . . . what happens when they are followed by such consequences takes us into the field of learning . . .' (p. 22). The acquisition and maintenance of fears is discussed in chapters 8 and 9.

During infancy, fearful reactions can be evoked by the range of stimuli described above – intense, sudden or novel stimuli – and for a time, unfamiliar people. With increasing age, the child's range of fears widens. He can recall past events and anticipate dangers; he can also respond to imaginative impulses and images, such as ghosts. As the child graduates to more complex fears, however, he also learns to cope with the earlier sources of fear and is less likely to fear sudden noises, for example. Fear responses of children at different ages were described by Jersild and Holmes (1935). They observed an overall change from immediate, tangible fears to anticipatory, less tangible ones with increasing maturity. For instance, most two-year-old children were found to respond fearfully to loud noises and to events associated with noise, whereas only a minority of six-year-old children were fearful. These older children were more inclined to fear imaginary situations. A fear of animals was present in nearly half of the children up to the age of six years and we also know that these animal fears begin to decline in middle childhood until in a group of fifteen-year-olds, less than 10 per cent were found to have retained this fear (Shepherd, Oppenheim and Mitchell, 1971). The fears of new situations and of noises show a marked decline during the third and fourth years of life and are present in only a minority of six-year-olds (see Figure 3). It is assumed that most noises cease to elicit fear because of habituation and, by the same token, the fear of new situations is gradually eroded in the course of the child's day-to-day experiences. Frequent exposures to new situations will either be followed by positive consequences or, more simply, the absence of unpleasant stimulation. Consequently they will tend to extinguish.

The general decline of fears with increasing age has been confirmed in a number of surveys (Rachman, 1968). The findings can be summarized as follows: the fears of young children are extensive; the majority of these fears undergo a steady natural decline; the quality of the fears changes from tangible to intangible with increasing age. There are some exceptions to these general trends and the fear of meeting new people and that of general shyness, show little decline during early and middle childhood. Shepherd, Oppenheim and Mitchell, found that slightly more than half of their sample of over 6000 children were described by their parents as continuing to demonstrate some fear of meeting new people and some shyness right into middle adolescence. In the same study, however, they were able to confirm that fears of darkness and of animals, present in nearly half of their five-year-olds, had markedly diminished in the older age groups. In an experimental investigation of the fluctuations of fears with increasing age, Holmes (1935) exposed more than fifty children between the ages of two and six years to several experimental situations of a potentially frightening character. The percentage

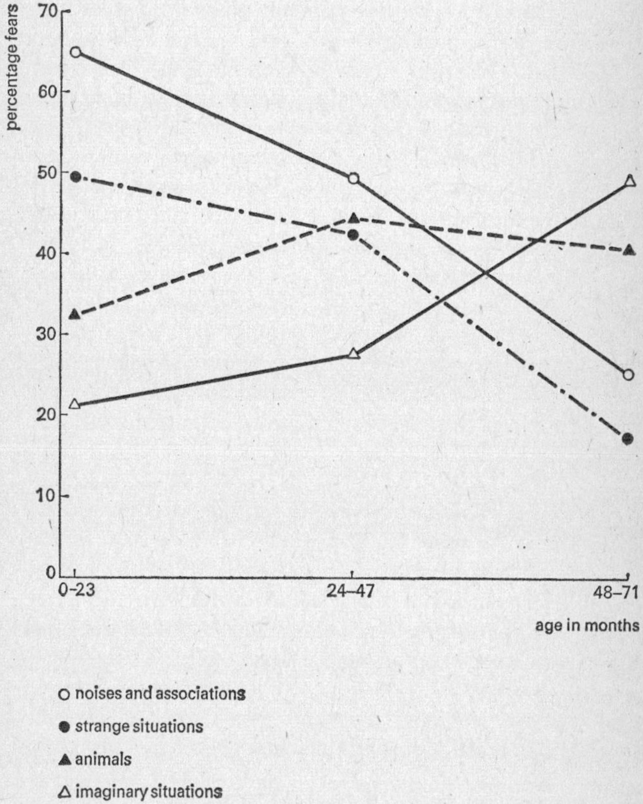

Figure 3 The course of some fears of childhood. Adapted with permission of the publisher from Jersild and Holmes (1935)

of children in whom fear responses were elicited by the presence of a strange person decreased from 31 per cent in the two-year-old group to 7 per cent in the four-year-olds and 0 per cent in the five-year-old group. Other examples include the fear of being in a dark room which declined from 47 per cent of two-year-olds to 0 per cent of five-year-olds, and the fear of being left alone which dropped from 12 to 0 per cent between the ages of two and five years. A microscopic examination of the decline of fear responses in young children was reported by Slater (1939). Forty two-year-old children were closely observed during their first four weeks of attendance at a nursery school. During the first week the majority displayed signs of uneasiness and apprehension, but by the end of the fourth week all but three of them had adapted successfully (see Figure 4).

Despite their widespread occurrence, children's fears rarely constitute a problem. In an intensive survey of more than 2000 ten- and eleven-year-old schoolchildren, Rutter and his colleagues (1970) found that 126 (5·7 per cent) had some psychiatric disorder. Of these children, only sixteen were found to have a clinically significant fear. The most common fears were of spiders (five cases) and of the dark (six cases). These children are part of that small minority who do not lose their fears of the dark and of insects or animals.

Persistence

The persistence of some fears throughout and beyond childhood is of interest in view of some recent findings by Marks and Gelder (1966) on the subject of neurotic phobic conditions in adults. They found that adult patients presented with circumscribed fears, especially of animals, reported having had the fear since childhood – these cases of abnormal persistence of childhood fears are uncommon and readily modified, but nevertheless pose theoretical problems. In the light of clinical studies, it can be expected that these fearful adults were more *generally* timid than their childhood peers and were possibly overprotected.

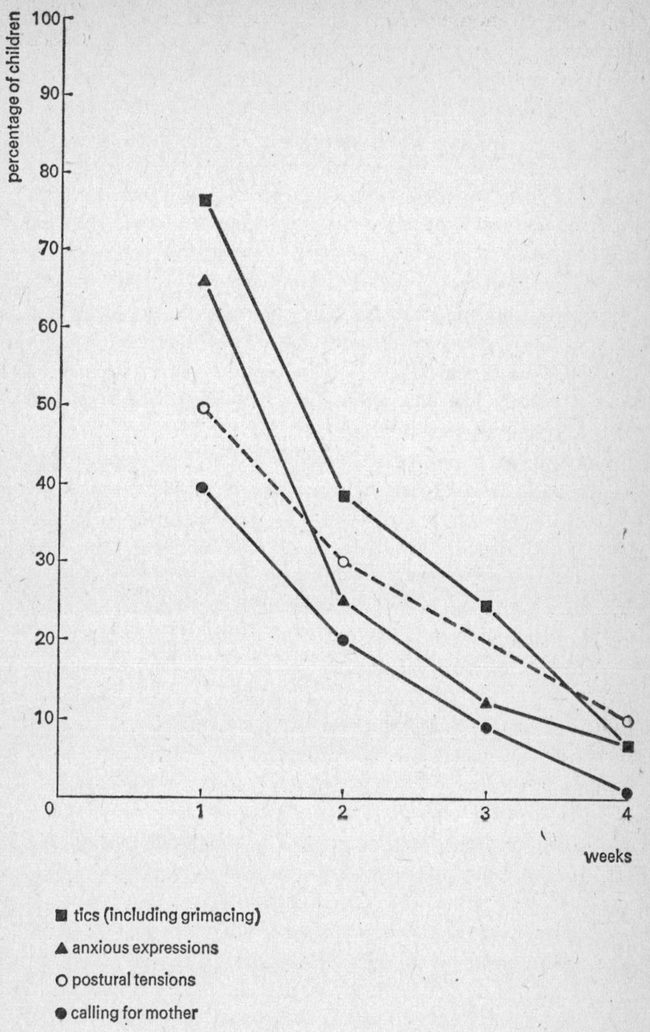

Figure 4 The decline of signs of fear in nursery school children during the first four weeks of attendance. Adapted from Slater (1939)

Viewed at another level, one might postulate that these people have an innate propensity to habituate to certain types of stimuli only after many repetitions under very special conditions. They do not, however, display a *general* failure to habituate to stimulation – in fact, they habituate rapidly to auditory stimulation (see chapter 9).

It is worth bearing in mind that, while the excessively long-term persistence of circumscribed fears (e.g. of animals) may well be associated with certain personality characteristics, these are *not* indicative of a general psychiatric disorder. On the other hand, the presence of multiple and diffuse fears shows a clear association with psychiatric disorders (see chapter 6).

Although it is not a sign of psychiatric disorder, the persistence of an excessive fear, even of a circumscribed type, can produce a degree of incapacitation. For example, a seven-year-old boy was referred for treatment because he complained of an intense fear of bees which had been disturbing him for the past two years. He described the subjective aspect of his reaction simply: 'I am very frightened of the bees and feel scared that they will sting and hurt me.' His mother described the external signs of her child's fear when confronted with the bee in this way: 'He used to go white, sweaty, cold and trembly and his legs were like jelly.' The child's motor reaction was one of avoidance, and where this was unsuccessful, blind flight. This apparently simple and unimportant fear had severely curtailed the child's range of movement. For instance, he was unable to play out of doors during the summer and had to be driven to and from school during spring and summer terms. On a number of occasions he had been unable to avoid coming into contact with bees and these experiences had produced intense fear reactions. The child's attempts to escape from bees had lead to a number of disturbing experiences which had finally prompted him and his parents to seek assistance. On at least two occasions he had run across busy streets when confronted by a bee and his parents were concerned lest he come to harm because of his intense, blind-escape reactions.

To summarize: it appears that we are born with a propensity to develop fears of intense, sudden or novel stimuli and certain types of social stimulation. During early childhood we display extensive fears which then undergo a slow natural decline. With increasing age, the quality of fears changes from tangible to intangible.

6 Types and Degrees of Fear

Research into ways of modifying fear has led to a demand (not satisfactorily fulfilled) for methods and instruments capable of describing and measuring the range and intensity of fears. To this end, Wolpe and Lang (1964) among others constructed fear inventories. The early version of Wolpe and Lang's scale was then developed and refined by other workers and applied to substantial groups of university students and selected groups of psychiatric patients. These inventories characteristically contain between 30 and 150 items, each referring to a range of objects and situations which are presumed to evoke a measure of fear in at least a proportion of the population. The subject is required to rate each item for the degree of fear which it usually arouses in him and for this purpose a five-point scale is generally employed – ranging from one, meaning no fear at all, to three indicating moderate fear and five indicating extreme fear.

The resulting pattern of fears can then be examined for clinical purposes. In the case of research, the item scores of a large sample of subjects are intercorrelated and subjected to factorial analysis in order to determine whether or not there are 'clusters' of fears. Typical items used in inventories of this kind include the following: sharp objects, germs, blood, feeling rejected by others, public speaking, snakes, deformed people, examinations and so on. As with all inventories, the results can only be a reflection of what is fed in by way of questions. Unfortunately, the chronic and diffuse types of fears are poorly represented, while the more episodic, acute and stimulus-provoked fears are over-represented.

Nevertheless, the results of investigations carried out predominantly on groups of American students have revealed some interesting findings. In all the factor analytic studies a fear of certain kinds of social situation or event emerges as a clear and strong factor. Similarly a fear of animals and/or insects is always present, as is a fear of harm/injury/loss. In addition, some other variations have been described, such as a factor denoting a fear of water, or a specific fear of death. The fears and factors observed in psychiatric samples bear similarities to those revealed in non-psychiatric groups, but tend to be more widespread and intense in the disturbed groups. Overall, psychiatric groups endorse a greater number of fear items and also rate their fears as being more intense than do subjects in non-psychiatric samples. It has also been found that the fear inventory scores show moderately high correlations with standard tests of general anxiety such as the Taylor Manifest Anxiety Scale. In addition to the general surveys of fear, some inventories have been constructed to tap specific types of fear such as public-speaking fears, test-taking fears and so on. Again, the total scores on these sub-scales tend to show a moderately high correlation with fear and anxiety scales of a general character.

In all the major investigations it has been observed that women express fears of more objects and situations than men and they also indicate higher degrees of fear. It has been suggested however, that this sex difference, indicating excessive timidity among women, may reflect the greater willingness of women to admit their fears rather than an accurate portrayal of the differences between men and women. Although there is sound evidence to support the argument that women will more readily admit to fears, the data on behavioural avoidance tests and physiological indices support the view that the reported sexual differences in timidity are authentic. It appears that female fearfulness is genuine and male fearfulness, although present and admitted, is partly disguised.

In a psychiatric sample studied by Lawliss (1971) it was found that the major fear factor concerned social situations,

The patients endorsed fears relating to the loss of approval, feelings of rejection by others, loss of status, humiliation and so on. In the same study, a second major factor was composed of items relating to fear of small animals and insects, such as snakes, spiders and rats. This factor is interesting because of its comparability to similar factors detected in populations of students, and because much of the research on the experimental and clinical reduction of fears has relied on subjects with circumscribed fears of animals and insects.

Abnormal fears

It need hardly be said that the fears expressed by psychiatric patients are not *ipso facto* pathological; the great majority are normal fears. The distinction between pathological fears (phobias) and normal fears does not rest on the clinical status of the fearful person. It is a distinction which is easy to draw when comparing the extremes of pathology and of fear, but which usually depends on shades of intensity. If, as seems unavoidable, the intensity of a fear is to be graded on a continuum, it comes as no surprise to find that a cut-off point between normal and pathological is difficult to determine. The difficulty does not preclude the need or suffocate the attempt, and pathological fears, or phobias, are generally defined as excessive fear reactions which are both persistent and unadaptive. All three of the key adjectives are of course relative terms and the definition happily assumes a unitary type of fear reaction. Despite these drawbacks, clinicians find some utility in the definition even if purists grimace.

All of the four components of fear described in chapter 2 are observed in moderate to intense degree among people with phobias. The subjective aspect of a phobia is experienced by the person as an alarming feeling of intense fear or panic and may be expressed in a variety of ways. Some patients for example, report that they feel as if they are dying; others feel that they are suffocating and yet others that they are going to faint or collapse. The bodily reactions include a combination of these feelings or responses: rapid respiration, sweating, trembling, palpitations, muscular tension or weakness, involuntary excretions, 'butterflies in the stomach', nausea, dryness of the mouth. In the grip of a phobic reaction, the patient may flee blindly, or may wish to do so, or he may become inert and feel incapable of movement. The facial and other manifestations of fear evident to other people include evidence of tension, staring, trembling, pallor and so on.

These various manifestations can be illustrated by reference to phobic cases, the most common of which are agoraphobia, animal phobias, social phobias, sexual phobias and phobias of being trapped.

Severe chronic agoraphobia is illustrated by the case of a forty-five-year-old man whose symptoms had persisted for ten years without much change. He complained primarily of an inability to walk about in public and of a strong fear of being alone at any time. When he attempted to leave his home unaccompanied he experienced a severe fear reaction which he described as a feeling that 'something dreadful was about to happen' to him. He had in fact experienced a number of panic attacks during which he felt that he was going to die (of a heart attack). The bodily reactions which accompanied these subjective feelings of apprehension included breathlessness, palpitations and feelings of weakness which forced him to support himself against the nearest wall. He tended to avoid a large number of situations and when he was induced by pressing demand to leave his home, he restricted his walking to those routes which he knew contained walls on which he could support himself if necessary. In practice, it meant that whenever he walked outside his home for any distance he was obliged to creep alongside a wall, touching it as he proceeded.

A medical student, who complained of an intense fear of figures in authority and of examination situations, described his feelings as bordering on panic whenever he was unable to avoid the presence of his teachers, senior colleagues and so on. He was quite unable to cope with these people, felt extremely frightened and trembled and sweated in a way that was clearly visible. The bodily reactions in his case were sweating, muscular tension, blushing and flushing and palpitations. In addition, the muscular tension often centred on the muscles of the throat region and this prevented him from speaking normally in the presence of authority figures. Whenever and wherever possible he avoided coming into contact with his teachers. This unadaptive behaviour was interfering with his education, apart from the heavy burden which it imposed on him in day-to-day matters affecting his social life.

A third example, of a sexual phobia, was that of a young girl who was frightened of pain and discomfort which might be induced by penetration of her vagina, either by the use of tampons or during intercourse. In both of these circumstances she experienced powerful anticipatory fears marked by gross trembling, sweating, and pallor, and sometimes her general feelings of bodily weakness were translated into fainting spells of short duration.

In his lucid guide to the clinical phenomena of phobias, Marks (1969) attempted a classification of the clinical phobic syndromes. The major categories are: social phobias, specific animal and insect phobias, illness phobias and agoraphobic disorders. In a survey carried out in a major psychiatric teaching hospital, he found that 60 per cent of the phobic cases fell into the category of agoraphobia. The social phobias were surprisingly under-represented by only 8 per cent of the total, but this may be a reflection of diagnostic practice rather than their actual occurrence in the psychiatric population. Various types of illness phobias accounted for 15 per cent of the sample, animal phobias comprised 3 per cent of the population and miscellaneous specific phobias comprised 14 per cent.

The animal phobias were confined almost entirely to women, had their origins in early childhood and showed a relatively unchanging course over many years. The agoraphobic group also showed a preponderance of women (75 per cent of the sample), with a later age of onset – generally after puberty. The condition tended to be associated with generally high levels of anxiety, depression and other symptoms. Although the disorder was found to persist for longer than a year in most cases, it did show fluctuations from time to time with periods of comparative freedom from fear. What is described as agoraphobia in clinical practice generally comprises a number of inter-connected fears, such as a fear of being alone, difficulty in leaving the home, fear of closed spaces, transport vehicles, social situations and so on. The social phobias show a much more even distribution between men and women and are characterized by fears of contact with other people in the form of social conversation, eating or drinking in public, speaking in front of strangers or a group of people. Like the agoraphobic disorders, social phobias tend to have their origin after puberty and usually emerge between the ages of fifteen and thirty. They are often associated with depression and occasionally with high levels of background anxiety. They show little fluctuation over the years. The intense fears of illness, which centre on specific diseases or disorders like cancer, venereal disease, cardiac disorders and so on, resemble certain other psychiatric disorders and are sometimes difficult to distinguish from them, for example, obsessions. These illness phobias occur with equal frequency in both sexes and tend to make their appearance in early adulthood.

The agoraphobic disorders, which feature prominently in most clinics, have been the subject of considerable research and a number of surveys. One of the most interesting of these was carried out by Marks and Herst (1970) on 900 female members of a voluntary association for agoraphobics called 'The Open Door'. The information was gathered by questionnaires, supplemented by interviews of a small number of subjects. Among this group the most common and intense fears reported were: speaking to audiences, riding in underground trains, crowds of people, travelling in buses or trains, heights, going to the hairdresser, streets and open spaces. Among the other problems reported by this group of patients were exhaustion, tension, obsessions, depression and loneliness. A quarter of them also complained of moderate to severe fears of disease, dying, fainting. Forty per cent of them complained of some sexual difficulty and a significant minority were so handicapped that they were unable to obtain or maintain employment. It is not clear whether agoraphobic disorders are precipitated by environmental stresses in a direct manner, if at all. Estimates of the importance which should be attached to the precipitating factors present at the onset of the disorder range widely. In the survey carried out by Marks a substantial number of agoraphobics reported that their major difficulties started after a significant change had occurred in their life – 'serious illness in patient or relative, acute danger or discomfort, leaving home, bereavement, engagement, marriage, pregnancy, miscarriage, childbirth ...' (p. 128).

Agoraphobias, like social phobias, occasionally have a specific focus, but more commonly the manifestations are diffuse. The fears of animals or insects are, with few exceptions, confined to the phobic object and variations on that theme. People with such phobias hardly ever complain of chronically high levels of anxiety or of incapacitation or inconvenience outside of those situations in which the animal or insect does or may feature. The fear may be thought of as having a confined focus. It is a curious fact that, despite their onset in early childhood and their unvarying persistence, these focal fears are more easily reduced or eliminated than the diffuse fears acquired in early adulthood.

Fear of death

In contrast to the considerable attention which psychologists have devoted to the study of tangible fears, little systematic research has been carried out into the nature of what are sometimes called existentialist fears. The shortage of information is well illustrated by the literature on the fear of death. Research into this profound problem has been characterized by what Lester (1967) describes as a 'lack of ingenuity'. He also points out that 'our understanding of this fear has increased very little compared to the progress in other areas of psychology.' The studies have relied on interviews or on simple questionnaire techniques and have yielded little information and most of it is in any event of a negative character. For example, the many attempts which have been made to relate fear of death to demographic variables such as age, occupation, income, urban or rural location and so forth have produced no correlations of any great interest. The potentially rewarding analysis of the relation between religious ideas and convictions, and attitudes towards death has so far not proceeded beyond superficial approaches. Two isolated findings that are worth noting *en passant*, are the greater preoccupation with death and fears of death which are expressed by women, and the finding that people who have completed a university education are better able and willing to discuss their conceptions and fears of death than are people who have not completed any form of higher education.

Lester has suggested that the unsatisfactory quality of presently available information about the fear of death is partly the result of a failure to distinguish between different aspects of the fear. He points out that earlier workers had argued successfully for a distinction to be made between a fear of one's own death, a fear of the death of others and a fear of the effects of death.

In his monograph on dying, Hinton (1967) distinguished between the fear of one's own death, other people's death and a fear of the dead or their spirits, and some support for these distinctions was later provided in a small study carried out by Collett and Lester (1969). They found that in a group of students the fear of one's own death and the fear of other people's death were uncorrelated ($r = 0{\cdot}03$). An important aspect of the fear of death is the expectation of pain and suffering and Hinton quotes a survey in which 90 per cent of the respondents expressed a desire for a rapid end, presumably in the hope of avoiding pain.

It should be remembered that a fear of death is not always recognizable as such. When closely analysed, many intensely frightening experiences, particularly those of a pathological type, are resolved into a fear of death. For example, numbers of patients who suffer from chronic and severe fears of being alone or of leaving the safety of their dens (agoraphobia) are most acutely aware of cardiac discomfort. When analysed frequently it is found to relate to or simply reflect a fear of death by heart failure. In cases of disease phobia, the connection with a fear of death is plain. In a group of psychiatric patients, Bianchi (1971) found excessive and irrational fears of cancer to be the most common disease-phobia (47 per cent), closely followed by the fear of heart disease (30 per cent). He reported that patients who suffered from these morbid fears were more anxious, moody and self-pitying than a comparable group of patients who had no phobias of disease.

A fear of death is of course neither universal nor unchanging. Numbers of people anticipate their own death with composure (longing for easeful death), and others seek a premature end by suicide. In some circumstances, one's death might be socially approved and feared less or not at all. The most obvious instances are seen in times of war and one of the most spectacular examples is that of the Kamikazis who eagerly volunteered for an honourable death.

In times of war, the social and personal pressures which are directed at the suppression of displays of fear provide an instructive example of the discrepancy between the various components of fear. Despite the presence of autonomic and other bodily feelings which are recognized as those of fear, the necessity to inhibit avoidance behaviour results in combat soldiers having to maintain themselves in contact with intensely frightening circumstances. The accounts given by Grinker and Spiegel (1945) of the experiences of air-crews during the Second World War show how the enormous social pressures maintained crews in intensely frightening missions despite the occurrence of subjective and physiological fear which often reached terrifyingly high levels.

Individual differences in fear

There are well-founded reasons for believing in the existence of substantial individual differences between people in the ease with which they acquire new fears and the persistence with which fears endure. Although it is possible, even likely, that the acquisition and endurance of fears are related characteristics, there is no certainty on the matter. The possibility that persistence of old fears may be a reflection of a slow rate of habituation to certain types of stimuli is a strong one, and it does not necessarily follow that slow habituators are the same people who readily acquire new and excessive fear reactions.

Individual differences in the acquisition of fears have received more attention than differences in habituation rate and attempts have been made to link fearfulness with other attributes of personality. One such major attempt has been made by Eysenck (1967) who has proposed that neurotic disorders can be incorporated within his two-dimensional model of personality. According to this scheme, the two major dimensions along which personality can be viewed are extraversion-introversion on the one scale and neuroticism on the other scale, at right angles to the first. This two-dimensional scheme has been the subject of a great deal of research and there is considerable evidence in its favour. The 'typical extravert' is out-going, sociable, impulsive, optimistic and so on. The 'typical introvert', on the other hand, is a quiet, introspective, cautious and serious person. The second major dimension, neuroticism, is akin to the description given by many other authors of emotional stability or instability. It is proposed that there are people whose emotional reactions are labile, intense and easily aroused, while at the other extreme there are those whose emotional reactions are more stable, weak and difficult to arouse. According to this view, neurotics would be expected to display the unstable and intense type of reaction pattern. Excessively fearful people and those with pathological fears in particular, can be expected to show a combination of high introversion and high neuroticism. Phobias are most likely to develop in people who are innately predisposed towards introverted patterns of behaviour and are at the same time endowed with a labile autonomic nervous system. It is to be expected that people who have this constitution will develop phobias earlier and more readily than either extraverts or people who are low on the neuroticism factor.

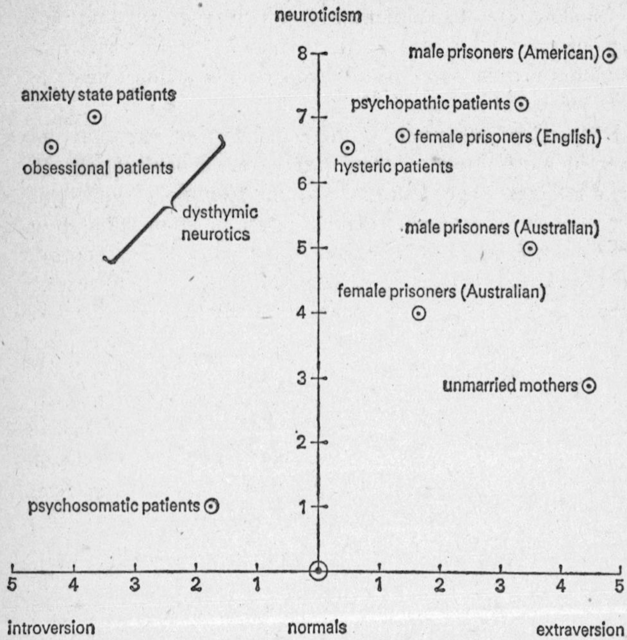

Figure 5 'The dimensions of personality', as proposed by Eysenck (1965)
Neurotic anxiety states, characterized by excessive fearfulness, are seen as a combination of high neuroticism and high introversion – upper left quadrant of the scheme

According to Eysenck's theory, the fearfulness of introverted people rests on the fact that they acquire conditioned responses more readily than extraverts under specifiable conditions. Extraverts acquire conditioned responses with difficulty, except under specific training conditions. In his recent book on fear, Gray (1971) attempted a reinterpretation of parts of the Eysenck theory: 'Eysenck's suggestion is that (the extravert) is bad at *conditioning*; my alternative suggestion is that he is bad at *fear*. That is, the extravert is relatively insensitive to punishment and the threat of punishment,' (p. 230). Gray's revision comprises two principal hypotheses. In the first place, he postulates that neurotic tendencies are correlated with high sensitivity to environmental events. The second postulate is that, 'increasing degrees of introversion represent increasing sensitivity to punishment rather than to reward'. Although his proposals undoubtedly have the effect of simplifying some complex phenomena and notions, the wider utility of Gray's theory will not become apparent until further research on the principal hypotheses has been completed. The lucid presentation of the theory ensures that experimental tests can be designed and conducted without difficulty.

7 The Reduction of Fear

Over the past twenty years impressive advances have been made in the development of techniques for reducing fear; in fact the techniques for *changing* fear have preceded a full study of the phenomenon itself.

The advances have occurred as part of a wider scientific movement culminating in new forms of psychological treatment which are collectively described as behaviour therapy (Wolpe, 1958; Eysenck and Rachman, 1965; Beech, 1968; Meyer and Chesser, 1970). The term *behaviour therapy* refers both to a group of techniques for treating a variety of psychological disorders and deficits and also to a new theory of psychological problems and their modification. Many of the underlying ideas and some of the methods of behaviour therapy are exemplified in the approach to the problem of reducing fear.

One of the most interesting antecedents of the current approach to fear reduction is found in the work of Watson and of Mary Cover Jones. Watson and Rayner (1920) gave details of their important demonstration of how a fear can be acquired. A young boy, Little Albert, was taught to fear a white rat and similar stimuli by repeatedly associating the appearance of a rabbit with a frightening loud noise (see page 78 below). With this work in mind, Jones in 1924 applied a conditioning method in order to overcome the fears of a three-year-old boy, Peter. The child displayed a fear of white rats, rabbits, fur, cotton wool and other stimuli of this type. As the fear of the rabbits appeared to be a focus of Peter's general fears, it was decided to reduce this one first. He was gradually introduced to contacts with a rabbit during his daily play period. He was placed in a play group with three fearless children and the rabbit was brought into the room for short periods each day. Peter's toleration of the rabbit was gradually improved. The progressive steps used in the process included: 'rabbit in cage twelve feet away tolerated ... in case four feet away tolerated ... close by in cage tolerated ... free in the room tolerated ... eventually, fondling rabbit affectionately'. Another method used by Jones involved the use of feeding responses. 'Through the presence of the pleasant stimulus of food whenever the rabbit was shown, the fear was eliminated gradually in favour of a positive response.' Using these techniques, Jones overcame Peter's fear of rabbits and all the associated fears. The follow-up of this child showed no resurgence of the fear of rabbits or related stimuli.

The similarities between Jones's method and more recent variations can be illustrated by reference to a case described by Eysenck and Rachman (1965). The seven-year-old boy with a phobia of bees described on page 48 above was referred for treatment. The phobia, which was intense and interfered with many of his activities (e.g. playing in the garden), had been present for three years. Although the boy could not remember having received a bee sting, he knew of several people who had been stung and/or had displayed excessive fear of bees. After a full investigation had elicited the nature of his fear, a list of fear-producing situations was compiled. The techniques chosen for overcoming the fear were feeding responses, social approval and gradual exposure to stimuli associated with bees. At first the boy was shown small photographs of bees and then he was assisted through the following stages: large photographs, coloured photographs, dead bees in a bottle at the far end of the room, dead bee in bottle brought gradually closer, dead bee out of the bottle, dead bee on coat, gradually increasing manipulation of the dead bee, introduction of several dead bees, playing imaginative games with the dead bees. The boy made gradual and systematic progress and after eight sessions he and his mother both reported a considerable improvement. His mother stated that he was 'very much improved ... he no longer had the physical reaction. He used to go white, sweaty, cold and trembling, and his legs were like jelly. He can now play alone in the garden quite comfortably.' A long-term follow-up showed no recurrence of the phobia.

Mary Cover Jones's prescience is shown by the fact that all five of her recommended methods for overcoming fear are used, in modern dress, in present-day clinics and schools. Pointing out that neither verbal reassurance nor disapproval are satisfactory methods of reducing fear, she recommended the five methods of: social imitation, feeding responses, systematic distraction, affectionate responses or direct conditioning.

Systematic desensitization

In recent times a major advance was recorded by a medical psychologist, Professor Wolpe, who carried out studies on the induction and treatment of experimental neurotic conditions in animals and then translated his findings into clinical practice. The fear-reduction technique which he developed for clinical purposes, *systematic desensitization,* has also found many applications in non-clinical settings. The technique of desensitization comprises two main elements: the subject is first given systematic training in muscle relaxation and, secondly, he is asked to imagine increasingly fearful scenes while in a state of calm relaxation. In practice, the technique involves the gradual and graduated imaginal presentation of fear-producing scenes, the nature or grading of which have been decided upon by subject and therapist in discussion. With repeated practice of the imaginal experience of the fearful scenes, the subject or patient gradually acquires the ability to tolerate the fearful ideas or scenes in his imagination and this improvement generally transfers to the real situation. Leaving aside for the moment the clinical value of desensitization, let us examine the contribution which it has made towards increased understanding of fear and its modification.

Analogue research

Much of our knowledge about fear has been obtained from the study of normal subjects who show an excessive fear of spiders, snakes, worms and the like (Rachman, 1967, 1971). Prompted by Wolpe's experimental reports and clinical accounts, Lang and Lazovik (1963) carried out an analogue experiment which became the model for a flood of similar studies on modification of fear. Their pioneer experiment, carefully designed and executed, was carried out on twenty-four snake-phobic students of Pittsburgh University. Each subject was chosen from a larger pool of fearful students, who in turn had been chosen from a still larger group of randomly selected students. The twenty-four experimental subjects were chosen not only on the grounds of their subjective estimates of their own fear, but also on the basis of their overtly observed fear in a behavioural avoidance test during which they were exposed to a live but harmless snake. Having ensured that their subjects were indeed excessively fearful, Lang and Lazovik divided them into two groups, one of which received desensitization while the other acted as a no-treatment control group. Each subject in the experimental group was given up to eleven sessions of systematic desensitization during which they were asked to imagine increasingly fearful situations involving snakes, while remaining in a deeply relaxed state. The control group subjects were given relaxation training and participated, like the experimental subjects, in the construction of a graded list of fear-provoking situations involving snakes. At the termination of the experimental treatment period both groups of subjects were reassessed and the results plainly showed that the subjects who had received desensitization were significantly less fearful of snakes than their control group counterparts. These reductions in fear were observed in both subjective and psychometric ratings as well as in the overt behavioural avoidance tests. Moreover, these changes were found to be maintained for at least six months when the follow-up investigation was carried out. In a subsequent study by Lang, Lazovik and Reynolds (1966). it was demonstrated that desensitization produces a specific change over and above any modification which might arise from the general therapeutic preliminaries or atmosphere.

In this second experiment, control subjects, who were given a cleverly designed form of pseudo-therapy, showed little change. It was also shown to be unnecessary for the experimental therapists to delve into the presumed basic causes of the subjects' fear of snakes. The development of a sympathetic relationship between the therapist and his subject was not sufficient to bring about changes in the fear of snakes. Lastly, their experimental results demonstrated that desensitization of a specific fear generalizes in a positive fashion to other fears and that modest all-round reductions in fear might be expected.

Virtually all of the conclusions reached by Lang and his colleagues have now been confirmed by other experimenters, using the same and different techniques, the same and different subjects, the same and different assessment procedures. The extent of the investigations and the surprising degree of agreement in their outcome has never been matched in any similar undertaking in abnormal psychology or its clinical applications (Rachman, 1967; 1971).

The rehearsal of fearful scenes in imagination, while in a state of relaxation, desensitization, has proved to be a robust technique for reducing fear. Numerous variations have been attempted in experimental studies – shortening the imaginal rehearsal time, abbreviating the number of training sessions, omitting to graduate the fearful scenes and so on – and in virtually all studies at least a moderate degree of fear reduction has been obtained. In addition to providing general support for Wolpe's work, research has also been directed at an exploration of the nature of the desensitization process itself. For example, several attempts have been made to isolate the effective elements in the procedure. Thus far the evidence suggests that the fear-reducing effects of desensitization are potentiated by the combined action of relaxation instructions and graduated presentations of fearful images. However, the role and action of muscle-relaxation training has been the subject of critical re-examination. Although muscle-relaxation training is likely to play a facilitative role in desensitization, it seems unlikely to be a prerequisite for the reduction of fear.

The experimental evidence on reduction of fear by desensitization can be summarized in this way. The imaginal rehearsal of graded fearful scenes effectively reduces fear; this process can be facilitated by relaxation. The reductions in fear are reflected in subjective reactions as well as by increases in overt approach behaviour – but less clearly or reliably by psycho-physiological indices such as skin resistance changes. The subjective and behavioural measures of fear correlate moderately well with each other, but slightly or not at all with psycho-physiological indices of change. The measures of fear reduction do not appear to change at the same speed. The usual sequence appears to be an increase in approach behaviour, followed by a decrease in subjective reports of fear.

It is unnecessary to ascertain the origin or putative symbolic significance of a fear in order to eliminate it. Neither is it necessary to change the subject's basic attitudes or to attempt to modify aspects of his personality in order to reduce his fears. The elimination of a fear, or a clinical phobia, is rarely followed by the appearance of new fears or substitute problems. The extent of the response to desensitization, that is the degree of fear reduction, is not related to the subject's suggestibility. Relaxation, alone, or accompanied by pseudotherapeutic interviews, does not reduce fears or phobias. The establishment of a sympathetic relationship with the subject does not of itself reduce the fear although it is possible that it might facilitate the process. Interpretive methods combined with relaxation reduce fear slightly or not at all.

Although presentations of imaginary fear-evoking scenes confer numerous practical advantages, there is good evidence to suggest that real-life exposures can be as or more effective, particularly if they are carried out in a graduated manner. We also have evidence that the reduction of fear by desensitization can be carried out as an automated procedure, and although the practical consequences of automation should not be underestimated, their theoretical significance is greater. Without necessarily discounting the possible contribution which a sympathetic therapist or experimenter might make in reducing someone's fears, it is plain that a wholly satisfactory explanation of desensitization effects must take into account the expendability of a therapist. Certainly any attempt to account for the fear-reducing effects of desensitization which relies wholly or largely on the personality or presence of a therapist is unlikely to succeed.

Although this book is not concerned with the clinical application of fear-reducing techniques, it is worth mentioning that desensitization, among other techniques of behaviour therapy, has been applied to clinical populations with some degree of success. Readers who are interested in the clinical effects of these techniques are referred to the books by Marks (1969), Eysenck and Rachman (1965), Meyer and Chesser (1970), Rachman, (1971).

Flooding

Within the last five years a new fear-reducing technique called *flooding* has been introduced into both experimental investigations and clinical practice. Although there are one or two variations on the main technique, the essence of flooding is that it involves the prolonged exposure of a fearful subject to intense fearful stimulation. The impetus for the development of this technique came largely from experimental investigations on small animals in whom fears were artificially engendered and then reduced by exposing them to the intense fear-evoking stimuli and preventing their escape. It was found that in many circumstances this exposure to high-intensity stimulation led to rapid reductions in fear. The introduction of flooding was also stimulated by the clinical work of an American psychologist Stampfl (1970) who developed a treatment technique called *implosive therapy*, in which patients were deliberately required to imagine scenes of great unpleasantness which were derived from the psychodynamic explorations carried out by the therapist. The material derived in this way was introduced into treatment and the person was asked to relive in his imagination distressing experiences of his past, particularly his childhood. Although the theoretical explanations proposed by Stampfl are unconvincing, some of the clinical effects which he reported gave rise to considerable interest and played a part in the development of the flooding technique. Flooding is usually carried out in real-life, although it can of course be presented to the subject in imagination only. After the subject and therapist or experimenter have determined the nature of the subject's most intense fears, he is exposed to them either in actuality or in imagination, for prolonged periods. This can result in a substantial reduction of fear and this outcome is usually obtained, when it is obtained, in a surprisingly brief period. The clinical effects of flooding are still under active investigation but the early indications (Rachman, 1971) are encouraging.

Therapeutic modelling

In view of the extensive and convincing evidence that desensitization is capable of reducing fear, any method which is claimed to produce results superior to those of desensitization bears close inspection. The first comparative experiment to give rise to such a claim was reported by Bandura, Blanchard and Ritter (1969). They reported that the technique of live imitation (modelling), followed by the fearful subject participating in approach behaviour, produced a significantly larger reduction in fear of snakes than did desensitization. This experimental report was remarkable for the magnitude of the change obtained by imitation (modelling) plus participation – in 92 per cent of the subjects the excessive fear of snakes was virtually eliminated. The practical application of imitation learning, usually called *modelling* nowadays, is also interesting for two other

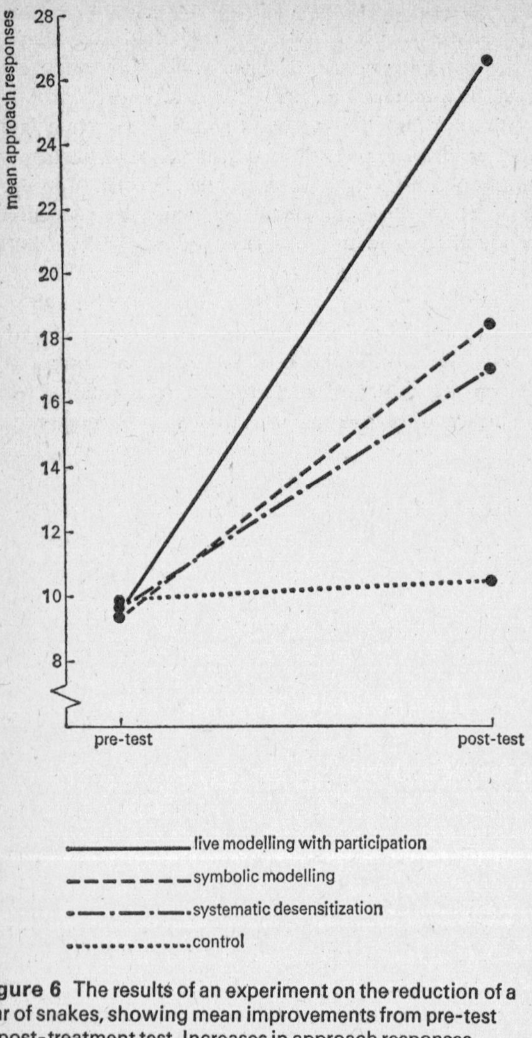

Figure 6 The results of an experiment on the reduction of a fear of snakes, showing mean improvements from pre-test to post-treatment test. Increases in approach responses are indicative of fear reduction. Both desensitization and modelling treatments were superior to the control condition and participant modelling was most effective of all. Reproduced from Bandura, Blanchard and Ritter (1969)

reasons. It was one of the two principal methods recommended by Mary Cover Jones in her 1924 paper – 'social imitation (in which) we allowed subjects to share, under controlled conditions, the social activity of a group of children especially chosen with a view to prestige effect' (p. 390). Moreover, in addition to its therapeutic value, imitation learning is of importance in attempting to construct a satisfactory explanation of the genesis and course of fear.

A good deal of the recent work is the product of Bandura and his colleagues who argue that modelling serves three important psychological functions. The models transmit new patterns of coping behaviour, prevent or interrupt unnecessary responses (including fear) and also facilitate the expression of previously learned adaptive behaviour. In consequence of his general theoretical position and also of his own research, Bandura has proposed the construction of a new therapeutic 'package' for dealing with fear. He recommends repeated modelling experiences, using multiple models whom the fearful subject can imitate and a progressive increase in the demands made on the subject. In addition, he argues that the imitation learning should be supplemented by repeated, real-life practice which incorporates the provision of guidance by the experimenter or therapist. By way of a general recommendation, Bandura urges that attempts should be made to arrange for the regular reinforcement of newly acquired fearless behaviour in order to ensure that it will endure.

Research into the fear-reducing power of imitation training has followed similar lines to that of research carried out with desensitization – and has had similar results. The present evidence can be summarized in this way (Rachman, 1972). Imitation training (modelling) produces significant reductions of fear under specified circumstances. This fear reduction is enduring and also generalizes to similar fear-evoking situations. The continuation of modelling by real-life practice of approach behaviour to the fearful situation will increase the extent of the fear reduction. It also seems probable that the therapeutic modelling effect is facilitated by repeated practice and by prolonged exposure times, both within a session and overall. The effect is also facilitated by the use of multiple models and the use of multiple fear situations or stimuli.

At this stage it would appear that there are two major determinants of the fear-reducing effects of modelling training. These appear to be the number of successful exposures to the model and the total time of successful exposures to the model. Of course it is not argued that modelling is a necessary condition for the reduction of fear, but rather that it can facilitate such reductions.

Naturally the introduction of another powerful method for reducing fear is entirely welcome. It does, however, raise some general problems which require explanation. For example, it may be asked why, if modelling is so successful in reducing fear, timid people do not automatically model fearless conduct in their natural environments? Why is it that the exposure to a model within an experimental or clinical context appears to achieve what has not been achieved elsewhere, despite the presence of other fearless models? There are several possible replies to these questions and all of them may have something to contribute to a final answer. In the first place, large numbers of people do in fact lose many of their fears in the natural environment. As we have seen in the section on children's fears, the great majority of these decline in middle to late childhood and certainly by the time of adolescence. Presumably part of the explanation for this natural disappearance of fear can be attributed to the spontaneous occurrence of repeated exposures to fearless models in the environment. An explanation for some failures of spontaneous fear reduction might rest with the fact that some people are repeatedly exposed to *fearful* models and, as we have already seen, children probably learn some fears through modelling their mothers. If a person has been repeatedly exposed to a fearful mother or other person, it is possible that he will continue to experience and manifest fear in a wider variety of situations than his peers. Lastly, some intense fears are not easily reduced –

by modelling or any other deliberate systematic procedure. Although it is too early to be sure, it seems probable that those people and those fears which are resistant to change will respond readily neither to desensitization, nor flooding, nor modelling.

The three fear-reduction methods

Method	*Description*
Systematic desensitization	Gradual and graduated Enhanced by relaxation and by *in vivo* practice
Modelling	Usually graduated Well suited to group administration and prevention Enhanced by *in vivo* participation
Flooding	Rapid exposure to the avoided stimuli When effective, results obtained quickly

Before embarking on an examination of the postulated explanations for the fear-reducing properties of these three techniques, it might be useful to recapitulate the findings on fear reduction in a brief, plain account. Leaving aside those pathological fears which require the assistance of a professional therapist, what are the simplest and most effective methods for overcoming or reducing fears?

The fearful subject should be exposed repeatedly to demonstrations of increasingly fearless approach behaviour, demonstrated by a model. After several repetitions of this passive form of modelling, the subject should be gradually integrated into the modelling exercises. That is, he should imitate the approach behaviour of the model in gradual and graduated steps until he is able to approximate the fearless behaviour himself. The model should provide feedback and encouragement in the course of his attempts at guided participation. In children, the process can be facilitated by the use of feeding and affectionate responses at critical stages in the learning process, particularly when hesitations occur. Another important technique for overcoming fears involves the rehearsal of increasingly fearless behaviour, either in imagination or actuality, preferably while the subject is in a calm state.

The reduction of pathological fears often requires the assistance of a professional therapist, although it is as well to bear in mind that roughly two-thirds of all neurotic conditions in which fear plays a prominent part, improve spontaneously within a two-year period (Rachman, 1971). Where professional assistance is obtained, it may take one of three forms, alone or in combination. Most frequently, tranquillizing drugs will be prescribed. Depending on the history and severity of the pathological fear and the general state of the patient, either psychotherapy or behaviour therapy might be recommended. The effects of psychotherapy continue to be a controversial issue and in the case of intensive treatment such as psychoanalysis, the patient is more likely to experience general improvement of a diffuse kind rather than a remission of the specific fears for which he initially sought assistance (Hamburg, 1967).

Desensitization is the most widely practiced of the behavioural methods and its success rate is reasonably high, particularly with fears of a circumscribed character. It generally requires between ten and thirty treatment sessions, comprising presentations of imaginary fearful scenes while the subject is in a state of deep relaxation, in order to achieve substantial reductions. The newly developed method of flooding is not fully understood, but the indications are that it will provide a more rapid alternative to desensitization – without a loss of effectiveness. Practically, the problem may well be one of obtaining the active cooperation of patients, although it must be said that early experience with this technique has been surprisingly free of problems. Given a choice between the slow, steady method of desensitization and the fast, uncomfortable method of flooding, the majority of patients appear to prefer the quick method. The therapeutic value of modelling has not yet been fully exploited but it is likely to prove useful, especially with children (Rachman, 1972).

8 Interpretations: Traumatic Conditioning

It has been shown in countless experiments that animals readily acquire fears. The evidence derived from these experiments, supplemented by naturalistic and clinical observations, led to the formulation of a theory which was intended to explain the genesis and spread of fears. Although originally conceived as a conditioning theory of fear, some limitations soon became apparent and the theory is more accurately described as a conditioning theory of *traumatic* fears.

The theory was developed over a period of a few years by Wolpe, Eysenck and Rachman and owes a good deal to earlier writers on the subject, particularly Pavlov, Neal Miller, Mowrer and Watson. The views of Pavlov and Watson appeared to be too narrow to accommodate the detail and complexities of the knowledge available in the 1960s and, although Mowrer's (1939) views were also overtaken in time, his clever and succinct analysis of fear as a conditioned pain reaction was enlightening. Miller and Mowrer, like Darwin and Freud before them, attached importance to the motivating quality of fears. Briefly, it was argued that the state of discomfort generally experienced in association with or as part of the fear, motivates the person to engage in correcting behaviour. Like Darwin, Mowrer and Miller both felt that the most effective forms of escape or avoidance behaviour would become fixed, according to some version of the law of effect (roughly, conduct leading to satisfaction will be repeated and that leading to discomfort or annoyance will not). They also recognized that, while fear is a motivating force which can act in a similar way to drives such as sex and thirst, it differs from these biologically based motives in that fear is *derived* from the basic states.

The major features of this theory were as follows: it was assumed that fears are acquired and that the process of acquisition is a form of conditioning. Stimuli or situations which are associated with a fear or pain-producing state of affairs develop fearful qualities; but some stimuli, by reason of their intensity or novelty, are more likely to acquire phobic qualities than others. It was also assumed that the strength of the fear is determined by the number of repetitions of the association between emotional experience and stimuli and also by the intensity of the fear or pain experienced in the presence of the stimuli. Conceived as a form of conditioning, it followed logically that stimuli resembling the fear-provoking ones would, by generalization, acquire fearful properties. The likelihood of fears developing is increased by confinement, by exposure to high intensity pain and/or fear situations and by frequent repetition of the association between the new phobic stimuli and the pain/fear. It was proposed further that once objects or situations acquire fear-provoking qualities, they develop motivating properties. This acquired motive was called the *fear drive*. Behaviour patterns such as avoidance actions, which successfully reduce fear, will increase in strength.

Evidence to support this theory was drawn from five main sources: research on the induction of fear in animals, the development of anxiety states in combat soldiers, experiments on the induction of fear in a small number of children, clinical observations (e.g. dental phobias) and some experiments on the effect of traumatic stimulation. Some of the clearest experimental examples of the induction of fear in animals come from the extensive literature on 'experimental neuroses', in which neurotic behaviour is artificially induced by conflict, frustration or other stresses (Wolpe, 1958; Broadhurst, 1960). In these experiments the animals display frantic avoidance behaviour or immobility, excessive trembling, crouching, restlessness, irritability, shallow breathing and the like. It has been found that once established, these manifestations of fear transfer to new and previously innocuous stimuli or situations.

In association with Rayner, Watson provided a classical demonstration of the development of a fear in a young child. Having first ascertained that it was a neutral object, Watson and Rayner presented an eleven-month-old boy, Albert, with a white rat. Whenever Albert reached for the animal, the experimenter made a loud noise behind him. After only five trials Albert began showing signs of fear in the presence of the white rat. This fear then generalized to similar stimuli, such as furry objects, cotton wool and white rabbits. These phobic reactions were still present when Albert was tested four months later. The demonstration made it clear that fears can be generated by a simple conditioning procedure in which previously neutral stimuli are associated with painful or frightening stimuli in such a way as to 'infect' the neutral stimulus. It was also seen that the phobic reactions spread without practice to other stimuli (generalization) which resembled the white rat in some manner. Some interesting corroborative evidence drawn from naturalistic observation was provided by English (1929). For example, a seven-month-old girl was observed to develop a fear of a black stuffed cat when its presentation was associated with an indignant scream from her older sibling. The infant had previously played quite happily with the cat and her fear response appeared to have been acquired by reason of association with the sudden loud noise – as in the case of Albert. However, English also made the point that other children continue to play happily with objects despite their repeated association with unpleasant stimulation. For example, a fourteen-month-old girl, Helen, continued to play with her painted wooden duck despite the fact that a loud noise was produced behind her head whenever she attended to the duck. Despite over fifty repetitions of this association, Helen did not register fear when the duck was presented. Along similar lines, Valentine described the fears observed in his own children and reported instances which seemed to follow the conditioning model.

On the other hand, some of his children displayed considerable resistance to the development of fears where they might, on the conditioning theory, have been expected. He put forward the idea that children have an intrinsic tendency to react fearfully to certain types of stimuli and to be resistant to other types of stimuli – a sort of hierarchy of phobic qualities among different types of stimuli. Discussing this topic, Marks (1969) argues that children are not born with a fear of specific objects but rather, 'they have a low threshold for showing fear to a few stimulus configurations which automatically lead to fear (of animals) under certain conditions', (p. 34). The idea that certain types of stimulation might be intrinsically likely to produce intense vigilance and even fearful reactions is also discussed by Gray (1971) in his interpretation of the evidence derived largely from animal research. As we have seen in chapter 5, the stimulus qualities which he feels are more likely to provoke intense reactions such as fear, are those which are novel, sudden, intense.

The observations and analysis of people under combat conditions provides ample evidence (Gillespie, 1945) of the production of intense fear as a result of traumatic stimulation. Grinker and Spiegel (1945) in their intensive study of American aircrews during the Second World War, gave vivid accounts of the fearful and disturbed behaviour produced by the stress of combat. Some of the fliers developed permanent feelings of intense apprehension, startled reactions produced by trivial sounds, uncontrollable tremors, marked tension, restlessness, nightmares and a host of bodily symptoms (diarrhoea, palpitations, nausea, headache, backache and so on). Another group of military veterans were asked to report which bodily symptoms they had experienced during the height of battle. The most commonly described fear reaction was palpitation of the heart, reported by two-thirds of the sample. The other prominent reactions were muscle tension (45 per cent), sinking stomach (44 per cent), dry mouth (33 per cent), tremor (25 per cent) and sweating (22 per cent). According to the analysis carried out by Grinker and Spiegel, the airmen suffered prolonged breakdowns that were precipitated by a single catastrophic event or were the result of exposure to severe, long-lasting, fear-provoking missions. Some of the airmen appeared to break down after *repeated*, prolonged exposure to moderately fearful situations – what one might describe as repeated sub-traumatic experiences.

From a study conducted on thirty-four cases of dental phobia (Lautch, 1971), we learn that every subject reported having had a traumatic dental experience (e.g. fearing suffocation when an anaesthetic mask was unexpectedly placed over the face) on at least one occasion in childhood. It is worth noting however that these thirty-four people were found to be *generally* neurotic while another ten comparison subjects who had experienced comparable traumatic incidents in childhood, showed little sign of neurotic tendencies. This suggestion of individual differences in reaction to traumatic or even simply unpleasant experiences, mirrors the findings of individual differences in predisposition to develop fear among different experimental animals.

A final source of support for the traumatic conditioning theory comes from some Canadian experiments in which subjects were given injections of a drug called scoline which produces a temporary suspension of breathing. Not surprisingly, most of the subjects who underwent this harrowing experience developed intense fears of anything connected with the experimental situation. In fact there was a tendency for the intensity of the fears to *increase* with time even in the absence of further unpleasant experiences – what Eysenck would call 'an incubation of fear'.

The need for revision

I hope that in giving this outline of the type and sources of evidence pertaining to the traumatic conditioning theory, it has been possible to convey the impression that there is a good deal to be said in its favour. Why then was it necessary to revise it? Although the theory has some merits, its applicability is limited (Rachman, 1968). Whatever its value, the theory is not a satisfactorily *comprehensive* account of the genesis and maintenance of fears. It had become apparent that 'clinically it is often difficult to determine the origin of a patient's phobia' (Rachman, 1968, p. 32). It can be extremely difficult to find a convincing precipitant of a phobia. Goorney and O'Connor (1971) encountered the problem in their analysis of excessive fears observed in peacetime aircrews. In a study of ninety-seven cases of excessive anxiety encountered in RAF crews, they were able to relate the fears of one quarter of all of their cases to specific precipitants such as accidents or frightening incidents. In one-third of the cases, however, there was no discernible cause and in the remainder, the precipitants were not of a traumatic or conditioning type, e.g. a return to flying after a long absence. A second and major weakness of the conditioning theory is that it has difficulty in accounting for the distribution of fears observed in the population at large. On the conditioning theory, most objects and environmental situations would have an equal probability of becoming fear-provoking, subject only to their prominence in the environment. What we find instead, however, is that some fears are exceedingly common – far too common for the theory. Other fears are far too rare. In the case of animal phobias, for example, one might expect that within a city population the fear of lambs should approximate that of the fear of snakes. In practice, of course, the fear of snakes is common and the fear of lambs is rarely encountered. To make matters worse, a genuine fear of snakes is often reported by people who have had no contact with the reptiles. Consequently one is forced to conclude that the fear of snakes can be acquired in the absence of direct contact – and this opens two prominent possibilities. Either the fear of snakes can be transmitted *indirectly* or, it is present but *not acquired*. While the possibility that a fear of snakes may be inherited cannot be ruled out, it seems more likely that there are certain stimulus characteristics which are readily transformed into fear-provoking stimuli.

A third difficulty for the conditioning theory arose from an unexpected quarter. In the course of administering and studying electrical aversion therapy, it gradually became apparent that few of the patients (sexual deviates and alcoholics for the most part) experienced or exhibited fear of the stimuli which had featured in the course of their treatment. Aversion therapy almost always involves the contiguous presentation of deviant stimuli and unpleasant, mildly painful electric shocks. On the basis of conditioning theory, one would predict that patients undergoing this form of treatment, particularly when the outcome was clinically successful, would develop a fear of the deviant stimuli which had been incorporated in the treatment and also of others which bore some resemblance to them. In practice, most patients become indifferent to the stimuli and very few become fearful of them (Rachman and Teasdale, 1969). One can even use these findings as a further example of the intrinsic differences between stimuli and the likelihood of their ever coming to serve as elicitors of fear.

A fourth and more constructive reason for revising the theory arose from the significant advances made in our understanding of the processes of observational learning and modelling (Bandura, 1969). It is plain that we acquire much of our behaviour, including emotional responses, by vicarious learning experiences. The confirmation of vicarious transmission of emotional behaviour opened the way to a valuable expansion of the theory. Recognition of this process helps to account for the skewed distribution of fears in the population (e.g. snakes *v* lambs). Partly no doubt because of its intrinsic qualities and largely because it is rarely seen to provoke fear, the lamb is seldom a cause of fear. On the other side, snakes are widely feared and widely seen to provoke fear. There are many opportunities for the social transmission of snake fears and of course, these opportunities do not require the presence of an actual snake. To this one may add the possibility that there are qualities in snakes which make them prepotent fear stimuli.

Taking all of these objections into account, one can either

substitute a new theory of fear or take the reformist course of revising the older version. This would involve an immediate extension and the possibility of another in due course. The essential revision requires the inclusion of vicarious transmission of fear. It is proposed (Rachman, 1968) that fears are acquired, either directly or vicariously; stimuli are likely to develop fearful qualities if they are associated, directly or vicariously, with painful or frightening experiences. The corollaries concerning generalization of fear, the effects of intensity and repetition and so forth, need no alteration at present. Before leaving the subject of the vicarious acquisition of fear, it is worth mentioning two pieces of evidence which provide indirect support. It was observed during the war that the fear or lack of fear displayed by mothers during the course of air-raids was the most important determinant of whether or not their children developed similar fears. Again, it has been found that there is a good deal of correspondence between the fears of children within the same family, with correlations ranging between 0·65 and 0·74 (May, 1950). Similarly, Hagman (1932) found a correlation of 0·67 between the total number of fears exhibited by children and their mothers.

The second revision of the theory concerns the assumption that all fears are acquired by environmental experiences. The possibility that some stimuli have intrinsic innate qualities which make them liable to assume fear-evoking properties cannot be ruled out.

At various points in this account of human fears, attention has been drawn to the tendency for fears to wane, and the term 'habituation' was introduced on several occasions to account for fear reductions. It refers of course to the fact that most responses will diminish in magnitude after repeated stimulation. Some responses however, persist despite the use of repeated stimulation. If we assume that this failure to habituate to certain classes of stimuli is closely related to fear, we may find a satisfactory resolution of the problem of innate fears.

We know that habituation to classes of stimuli which are

intense, novel or sudden is slow and/or incomplete (see, for example, Mackworth's lucid account, 1969). We also know that similar classes of stimuli (i.e. intense, sudden and novel) are common elicitors of fear (see Gray, 1971). If we combine these observations, a simplified view of innate fears becomes feasible.

Sudden, intense and novel stimuli may produce fear reactions; these reactions will wane on repeated presentation of the stimuli – with some exceptions. This means that in childhood, sudden, intense or novel stimuli (such as those produced by dogs, for example) will provoke fears. With repeated presentations of dog-associated stimulation, the fear of dogs will wane (at roughly three to five years of age). Now, the stimuli associated with dogs produce fear because of their attributes of intensity, suddenness and novelty and these are, of course, capable of provoking fear in any child old enough to perceive them satisfactorily (say from two months on). So we find a situation where most infants exhibit fears of some animals, even in the absence of any acquired association between the animals and pain or unpleasantness. The fear of some animals is not acquired in the sense implied in the conditioning theory; it is not a learned fear but an *elicited* fear. The prepotent fear stimuli are those which have the attributes of novelty, suddenness and intensity.

To recapitulate, fears are acquired by a learning process or elicited by specifiable stimulus combinations.

Thus far we have dealt largely with the development of fear. Mowrer (1939) put forward the notion that fear motivates the organism to escape and those responses which bring about a reduction of fear are reinforced or strengthened. This process can be illustrated by reference to the neurotic condition known as agoraphobia. Here the patient might have undergone a painful or frightening situation while in a public place (e.g. feels that he is having a heart attack), and on subsequent occasions will again experience tension and discomfort when he approaches the area of the first attack of unpleasantness. This anticipation of a further unpleasant experience can be regarded as a conditioned, anticipatory fear and it arises and increases whenever one approaches the original situation or indeed one which resembles it. The mounting fear then impels the person to make various attempts to avoid, contain or eliminate the fear. In the case of an agoraphobic, the action which most often brings relief is a return to the safety of the home. On his arrival home the patient generally experiences a reasonably quick dissipation of the fear and this relief then strengthens his tendency to retreat on subsequent occasions. In other words, the response of returning home is reinforced because it is followed by a reduction of the fear drive. The operation of this process in neurotic disorders was elaborated by Eysenck and Rachman (1965) who attached critical importance to the role of the fear drive in maintaining neurotic phobic behaviour. They argued that

> neurotic behaviour patterns persist paradoxically, because they are unpleasant. Once he has acquired an unpleasant reaction to a particular situation, the person then tends to avoid contact with that situation. As learned patterns of behaviour can only be extinguished by repeated, unreinforced (or inhibited) evocations, the tendency to avoid the noxious situation often precludes the spontaneous disappearance of the neurotic behaviour.

Although portions of this explanation, including the last statement about the conditions under which behaviour can be extinguished, need to be qualified, the notion that avoidance and escape behaviour is sustained by the operation and reduction of a 'secondary' fear drive still has utility. We now know, however, that it is not universally applicable and there are instances where fear is observed to persist even in the absence of escape or avoidance behaviour and contrariwise, avoidance behaviour persists even after the disappearance of fear. Although a number of attempts have been made to explain the occurrence of the exceptions, none of them has yet achieved wide acceptance.

9 Interpretations: Habituation and Sensitization

At various points in this book, reference has been made to examples of fears which appear to undergo *habituation* – in the sense of showing a decrement after repetitive exposures to fearful stimuli. The habituation of fear responses can be called upon to help account for the decline of childhood fears, phobic complaints, combat and parachuting fears and so on.

In the discussion of innate and acquired fears it was suggested that innate fears reflect an inborn tendency to respond persistently and intensely to objects or situations with certain stimulus attributes (e.g. novelty, intensity, suddenness). It assumes a heightened sensitivity to particular stimulus complexes. In her account of the phenomenon, Mackworth (1969) observed that habituation comprises a decrease in sensitivity to stimulation *and* a decrease in readiness to respond. Viewed in habituation terms, therefore, we can regard the fading of innate fears (as in childhood) as a decline in sensitivity observed after repetitive exposures to the stimulus. Decreasing readiness to *respond* is often an expression of this declining sensitivity.

The spontaneous decline of acquired fears can also be regarded as a function of repeated stimulus exposures, leading once again to a decreasing readiness to respond fearfully – a form of habituation. It is assumed here that these decremental processes, decreasing sensitivity and decreasing readiness to respond, are closely related but not identical.

In their interesting exposition, Groves and Thompson (1970) have argued that habituation comprises two *independent* processes. The first of these is the commonly recognized one of habituation resulting from repetitive stimulation and the second is what they describe as an incremental or sensitizing process. This sensitizing process refers to increases in responsiveness as a result of stimulation. They assume that habituation and sensitization develop independently but interact to yield 'a final behavioural outcome'. The fate of this theory will be watched with interest and it would be premature to extract the significance for our understanding of fear until the theory has been adequately tested. For the present, however, it is sufficient to recognize that habituation comprises a decrease in readiness to respond and a change in sensitivity and that furthermore, the possibility exists that these two processes are involved to different extents in the decline of innate and of acquired fears.

The occurrence of habituation, and indeed in the Groves and Thomson theory, of sensitization as well, is determined by a complex interaction between the subject's level of activity and the occurrence of repeated stimulation. The complexities of this interaction and the general characteristics of habituation are admirably described and explained by Mackworth. Following hers and Thompson's account, it will be seen that there is a great deal of common ground between habituation processes and factors which determine the reduction of fear in experimental and clinical situations.

The factors which facilitate habituation strongly resemble those which facilitate the experimental reduction of fear. The repetition of stimulation facilitates both habituation and fear reduction. The use of depressant drugs facilitates habituation and fear reduction, as does a lowering of the subject's level of psychophysiological activity. Other factors which facilitate habituation, and probably fear reduction as well, include an increase in the rate of stimulation, attenuation of the stimuli, regularity of stimulus presentations and reduced complexity of stimulation. There are other factors which enter into the development of habituation and of course, the ones mentioned above are all operative when other factors are equal. Leaving aside these qualifications, if we attempted to develop a technique for reducing fear which was based on present knowledge of the habituation processes, what would it look like?

Firstly, one would attempt to reduce the subject's level of psychophysiological activity. Then one would present the fearful stimuli in an attenuated form, repetitively, regularly, frequently – in simplified form – and possibly administer a suitable depressant drug.

The surprising thing about this hypothetical habituation treatment is the extent to which it resembles Wolpe's desensitization treatment technique. However, the two concepts developed independently and it was not until 1966 that Lader and Wing first proposed that the desensitization technique might profitably be conceived of as a form of habituation.

They suggested that desensitization was a form of habituation training, involving as it does the repetitive presentation of attenuated (fearful) stimuli. They proposed further that the effect of the relaxation training was to lower the subject's level of psychophysiological activity and thereby ensure more satisfactory and quicker habituation. In their own words, desensitization can be 'more simply regarded as straightforward habituation carried out when the habituation rate is maximal, i.e. with the patient at as low a level of activity as possible'. They arrived at this proposal as a consequence of their own research into factors which influence habituation and their experience of treating patients by desensitization. Later, their argument was bolstered by experimental evidence which bore directly on the hypothesis (Lader and Mathews, 1968). One of the most interesting pieces of evidence was the discovery that there is a significant correlation between habituation rate in certain laboratory test conditions and the response to treatment of various types of phobic patients. Broadly speaking, it was found that those patients who are slow to habituate are likely to respond less well to desensitization treatment than those patients who habituate easily and quickly.

Lang, Melamed and Hart (1970) obtained corroborative

evidence from samples of non-psychiatric subjects. Those people who had a fear of public speaking showed slow habituation to auditory stimulation (like Lader's patients with social fears), while the spider-phobics resembled Lader's patients with circumscribed phobics in showing easy habituation. In a later experiment, Lang (1970) obtained even more persuasive evidence in support of the habituation theory. Under specified experimental conditions, high correlations between habituation to short films of snakes and to auditory tones were recorded from snake-phobic subjects.

The theory has an appealing simplicity and is capable of generating specific and clear predictions. It is not without difficulties, however, and they include the following. The durability of habituation effects has not been clarified and the assumption that each person has a *general* rate of habituation, and that this can be accurately measured, is a notion which requires experimental support. The habituation model also has some difficulty in accounting for the persistence of certain circumscribed fears. In terms of the Lader–Wing hypothesis, patients with these specific fears should have a low level of physiological activity and consequently, habituate rapidly. It is difficult to see therefore why naturally occurring habituation does not wipe out these often long-standing fears (e.g. of birds, heights, etc.). The technical problems of specifying, in advance, what is a satisfactorily low level of activity, or indeed an unsatisfactorily high level, may in the long run reduce the value of the theory. Lastly and perhaps most important of all, it seems unlikely that the habituation model would have been able to predict the successful results of the flooding technique for reducing fears.

Wolpe's (1958) own explanation of the fear-reducing effects of desensitization is somewhat different. It is based on a concept called reciprocal inhibition, borrowed from physiology. He argues that the therapeutic benefits of desensitization derive from the repeated evocation of small amounts of fear and their immediate suppression by relaxation, it being assumed that there is an incompatible relationship between fear and relaxation. Whenever, during the course of desensitization treatment, the therapist evokes a small amount of fear in the patient and then suppresses it by encouraging deep relaxation, a contribution is made to a long lasting or permanent reduction of fear. Each piece of treatment comprises another block which goes towards the construction of enduring fearlessness. There is a good deal of evidence to support Wolpe's theory. It has been found in some studies that the desensitization method will only produce substantial reductions in fear if the repeated presentations of imaginary fearful stimuli are accompanied by deep relaxation. These findings support Wolpe's idea of a necessary interaction between fear experiences and their suppression by relaxation. It has also been found that fearful subjects who relax well and obtain clear and evocative images on instruction will show the greatest improvement after desensitization.

On the other hand, some experimental findings are not consistent with the theory. For example, it has been found that the omission of relaxation does not necessarily prevent the reduction of fear. It has also been observed that, at crucial points, Wolpe's theory is not sufficiently explicit and moreover his attempt to draw an analogy between a physiological process of inhibition and a psychological one is not entirely satisfactory. Despite the fact that fear and relaxation are known to be incompatible in many circumstances, this is not universally so – for example, sheer muscle relaxation does not preclude the experience of subjective fear.

Neither Wolpe's theory nor Lader and Wing's habituation hypothesis can accommodate the recent findings on the fear-reducing effects of flooding techniques. Certainly, neither of the theories could have predicted the outcome of recent research. In consequence, the theories will have to be modified and extended or it can be argued that we are dealing with processes which are so different that they require entirely separate explanations. It is too early to decide on these complex matters, largely because there is a shortage of critical information. It is also possible of course that our increased understanding of fear and its reduction may in turn lead to modifications of the prevailing conceptions of habituation and inhibition processes. Can one achieve rapid habituation by prolonged exposure to intense stimulation – as in flooding of fear responses?

The fear-reducing effects of modelling procedures raise fewer theoretical complications than flooding. There are many obvious similarities between modelling and desensitization (repeated exposures to attenuated fear stimuli) and in fact the most prominent theory to account for modelling effects (Bandura, 1969) has features which resemble both Lader's and Wolpe's ideas. Bandura's distinctive contribution has been the emphasis which he places on cognitive factors and on the undoubted occurrence of fear-reduction by vicarious means. Simply watching a suitable model engaging in fearless behaviour will lead to a partial reduction in one's own fear.

Another possible candidate for a unitary explanation of all three fear-reduction methods – desensitization, flooding and modelling – is reinforcement theory, along the lines described by Skinner (1953). Although this theory has attractive aspects, it falls short in some respects and most notably in the case of symbolic modelling effects. It also has difficulty in accounting for the fear-reducing effects of automated desensitization (Rachman, 1972).

If this chapter on interpretations of fear reduction leaves one with a feeling of incompleteness, this is both understandable and desirable. The major problems cannot be resolved at present. There are many appealing and clever ideas current, none of them wholly adequate, and a shortage of critical information. Each year brings advances in identifying the types of information which are required. So far, the borders of the jigsaw puzzle have been established.

10 Interpretations: Psychoanalytic Views

Psychoanalytic writers and academic psychologists do not merely give different accounts of fear; on critical points they are in direct conflict. A clear example of one such disagreement and its important practical consequences, is seen in the way that they view the fear of animals and insects. As described in chapter 7, more than fifty experimental studies on the desensitization of fear have now been published. With one or two exceptions, it has been found that desensitization successfully reduces fear. In the great majority of these experiments, the focus of study has been either a fear of spiders or a fear of snakes and consequently a great deal of information about these fears is now available. Broadly speaking, most of the experimental psychologists who carried out these investigations would adhere to the theory that the fears have been acquired, either directly or vicariously, and that furthermore, the fears are subject to relearning or unlearning by means of desensitization or related learning techniques.

In contrast, psychoanalytic writers regard these fears as the overt manifestations of some more profound underlying fear, usually of a sexual nature. Reference to two contemporary contributions will illustrate the complexity of the sexual symbolism which is a central feature of psychoanalytic theorizing on the subject of fear.

Melitta Sperling, writing in the *Journal of the American Psychoanalytic Association* in 1971, pointed out that 'most investigators seem to agree that the spider is a representation of the dangerous (orally devouring and anally castrating) mother, and that the main problem of these patients seems to centre around their sexual identification and bisexuality,' (p. 493). Developing these ideas, she writes 'it is my contention that the choice of the spider symbol indicates a fixation to the pregenital and in particular to the anal-sadistic phrase in a very ambivalent and predominantly hostile relationship to the mother, with an inability to separate from the hated mother,' (p. 494).

The depth and seriousness of a fear of spiders is plain.

> The spider symbolism as well as the symptoms most frequently found associated with it, such as severe sleep disturbances and phobias, are also an indication of unresolved separation conflict and a high degree of ambivalence which intensifies bisexuality and the problem of sexual identification. The mechanisms of defence employed in spider symbolism and in phobias are denial, externalization, projection, splitting and displacement. They indicate the primitive, ambivalent, narcissistic ego organization of this phase. The personalities of these patients and in the mothers in cases where it was possible to study them, showed marked paranoid trends. They also used psychosomatic symptoms in stress situations, either episodically or more persistently for the immediate (somatic) discharge of threatening impulses. The spider symbolism in most cases remained latent and became manifest in traumatic life situations and in analysis when the phobic and psychosomatic defences were invalidated. In the analytic situation the spider symbolism was indicative of a specific mother transference (p. 497)

The puzzling part about all this is that, despite the presence of this demoralizing array of problems – bisexuality, anally castrating mothers, primitive egos, paranoid trends, psychosomatic symptoms, and the rest – a fear of spiders can be desensitized within three to five sessions.

It would seem from Sperling's account that the adoption of a spider fear is to be regarded like other fears, as a form of psychological defence against some more threatening problem or impulse. Hence, 'the spider symbolism in most cases remains latent and becomes manifest . . . when the phobic and psychosomatic defences are invalidated.' If, as seems reasonable, one were to consider the reduction or entire elimination of a spider fear during desensitization as 'an invalidation' of a 'phobic defence', then the spider symbolism should presumably be made manifest by this change. In none of the experiments referred to have such dramatic changes been observed. On the contrary, the whole process of desensitizing the fear of spiders and other creatures is bland, unsurprising and at times boring.

Like Sperling, Newman and Stoller (1969) were greatly influenced in their approach to spider fears by the views of one of Freud's closest associates, Karl Abraham, who wrote a classic paper on the subject in 1922. According to him, the fear of spiders is symbolic of the unconscious fear of bisexual genitalia – 'the penis embedded in the female genitals'. The second meaning which Abraham attributed to the spider is that of a phallic, wicked mother. In their contribution to the *Journal of the American Psychoanalytic Association* in 1969, Newman and Stoller supported Abraham's view and illustrated it by reference to a psychotic patient who was physically deformed and had hermaphroditic genitalia.

Most of the psychoanalytic writing on the subject is speculation prompted by observation of one or a small selection of patients with a common problem. The difficulties which face one in attempting to evaluate this work will be gone into presently. For the moment it is worth pointing out that, even if Abraham and his successors are entirely correct in their assumption that a fear of spiders is symbolic of a fear of bisexual genitalia and/or of a phallic, wicked mother, there is room for optimism. As noted above, fears of bisexual genitalia and wicked mothers are capable of being desensitized readily and quickly.

Classic case

Freud (1905) laid the foundations for a psychoanalytic theory of fears with the publication of 'The analysis of a phobia in a five-year-old boy', commonly referred to as the case of Little Hans, the boy who feared horses. The importance of this contribution is attested to by Ernest Jones, Glover, Abraham and other writers on the subject. One of Freud's most famous papers, it describes and discusses in great detail (over 140 pages) the events of a few months. The case material on which the analysis was based, was collected by the father of Little Hans who kept Freud informed of developments by regular written reports. In addition the father had several consultations with Freud concerning the boy's fear (it should be mentioned here that both of the parents were lay adherents of psychoanalysis).

During the analysis Freud saw the little boy only once. The bare bones of the story are that at the age of four, Hans began to complain of a fear of horses. Shortly afterwards he appeared to show some degree of generalization to fears of other large animals such as giraffes and to objects which resembled a horse's muzzle. During a two-week illness the fear waned but then returned in a slightly more intense form only to show a gradual decline during the course of the succeeding six months. During the period when he complained of the fear, Hans was engaged in repeated conversations and interrogations by his father who then communicated his interpretations to Freud. The case material on which Freud's extended account is based and which provided the raw material for a theory of fear was almost entirely third-hand – and the reporter was himself a central figure emotionally involved in the matter.

Naturally the theory has undergone some revisions but the major propositions set out by Freud are still accepted by numbers of psychoanalytic writers. It is assumed that the observed or reported fear, the *manifest* fear, is symbolic of a deeper but more threatening or unacceptable fear; the underlying or *latent* fear is, with rare exceptions, sexual in nature. The latent fear is so threatening or unacceptable that it is unconsciously transformed into a more acceptable fear, such as that of spiders or snakes or horses. It is a means of defending one's self against more serious psychological disturbance and the mechanisms involved are those of denial, reaction formation, displacement and repression, among others. The fear is generally precipitated by an increase in *id* impulses.

Returning to the case of Little Hans, the boy's fear of

horses was interpreted as being a symbol of a more serious latent fear – in his case, as in so many others, a fear of his father engendered by anticipation of punishment (probably castration) for having experienced sexual desires for his mother. It can be seen that the fear of horses was interpreted as being a manifestation of the child's Oedipus complex: Hans experienced a sexual desire for his mother, followed by a fear of retribution from his father. These thoughts were unacceptable and the fear of the father was transformed into a more acceptable manifest fear, that of horses.

The full report has been discussed at length by Wolpe and Rachman (1960) who conducted a critical examination of the evidence on which Freud relied. They concluded that much of the testimony was unreliable, pointing to the fact that the child had demonstrably misled everyone on several occasions, that he gave conflicting reports and most important of all, that what purports to be Hans's views and feelings are simply the father speaking. Freud conceded that, it is true that during the analysis Hans had to be told many things which he could not say himself, that he had to be presented with thoughts which he had so far showed no signs of possessing and that his attention had to be turned in the direction from which his father was expecting something to come. This detracts from the evidential value of the analysis but the procedure is the same in every case (Freud, 1905, p. 246).

The critics quote several examples in which the child's reports were distorted, misinterpreted and even constructed for him. Wolpe and Rachman dispute each of the six major points put forward by Freud in the construction of his theory. They regard as unsupported the following contentions: the child had a sexual desire for his mother, he hated and feared his father and wished to kill him, his sexual excitement and desire for his mother were transformed into anxiety, his fear of horses was symbolic of his fear for his father, the purpose of the illness was to keep him near his mother, and finally, his phobia disappeared because he resolved his Oedipus complex.

The debate on the strengths and weaknesses of psychoanalysis has occupied armies of writers, psychologists, psychiatrists and others. The questions involved are complex and, if worried through to the end, lead inevitably to considerations of a philosophical nature. In particular it becomes necessary to make up one's mind about the nature of scientific methodology and evidence.

My view is that the crucial reliance given to the verbal testimony of subjects (many of them psychiatric patients), gathered over a vast number of treatment sessions extending across several years, is misplaced. The interpretation and selection which are necessarily involved in the report finally given by the psychoanalyst concerned should also be regarded with caution. The absence of public demonstration, repetition and accountability undermine one's confidence in the evidence. Many of the fundamental theoretical propositions of analysis seem to be inadequately based. In consequence of these reservations one becomes unwilling to accept the view that observed and reported fears are merely manifestations of a more fundamental, latent fear. Further, it is hard to see why one should accept the assumption that virtually all fears are manifestations, direct or indirect, of sexual problems and conflicts.

It would also appear that the recently accumulated evidence on the reduction of fear among experimental subjects by desensitization and related techniques poses tricky problems for psychoanalytic theorists. Manifest or latent fears can be readily reduced or eliminated.

Following the psychoanalytic view, the elimination of what is presumably a manifest fear (of spiders for example) should leave the latent fear unaltered. But, if it is assumed (and it is) that the appearance of a manifest fear is part of a psychological defence reaction, then it is only reasonable to expect that the elimination of the defensive reaction should be followed by some other attempt at defence.

Simply, it is reasonable to predict that the elimination of one manifest fear should be followed by substitution of a new one or failing that, by the occurrence of some other, perhaps worse, psychological disturbance. These two prime possibilities have in fact been explored in the experimental studies described in chapter 7.

After the successful reduction of a circumscribed fear such as that of snakes, the appearance of a new fear is rare. Secondly, after the successful reduction of one of these fears, the appearance of some general disturbance, perhaps diffuse anxiety or depression, is also rare. The evidence is straightforward. In the overwhelming number of cases the reduction or elimination of a circumscribed fear is not followed by untoward effects.

Another important consequence of the research findings on reducing fear is the conclusion that it is possible to bring about substantial reductions in fear without first undertaking a major analysis of the fear itself or of the subject's personality, childhood, sexual life or other topics which play such an important part in psychoanalytic theory. It is perfectly possible to approach the fear directly, describe and measure it directly, desensitize it directly – and with success. In other words, one can proceed on the assumption that the fear is manifest and need not have latent roots.

Does this mean that there are no 'psychoanalytic' fears? Not necessarily – for it remains entirely possible that many fears are partly or largely symbolic and it is of course the case that numbers of fears are implicitly or explicitly sexual in content. There is no way of estimating the frequency with which 'psychoanalytic' fears are encountered, but on present evidence it is likely that only a small percentage of human fears fall into this category. In my view then, the psychoanalytic theory cannot hope to succeed as a comprehensive account of human fears. It may help ultimately to understand a number of unusual fears.

It is a pity that psychoanalytic writers have not yet attempted to apply the 'multi-component' notion of fear to aspects of their theories. Is it possible in some way to link discordances between subjective and autonomic indices of fear to analytic ideas of *unconscious* fears? Is autonomic disturbance without subjective fear-recognition an instance of unconscious fear? Some interesting possibilities open up.

Although it might be agreed that psychoanalysis cannot provide a satisfactory general theory of fear, the voluminous literature on sexual fears and on symbolism contains many fascinating ideas. Unfortunately their successful exploitation is hindered by claims of exaggerated generality. All spider fears are symbolic of bisexual genitalia, all snakes are phallic symbols, and so it goes on. The implausibility of these claims too easily prompts a total rejection of symbolism, but neither total rejection nor total acceptance are comfortable positions to defend. Fears are not always exactly as they seem, but contrary to psychoanalytic beliefs, it is unwise to assume that fears are *never* as they seem.

11 Adaptive Fear

The adaptive value of fear has been emphasized by Lazarus (1966) among others. Most important, the arousal of fear stimulates a search for means of coping with impending difficulties or dangers. It is also known, however, that excessive fear impairs psychological functioning (Eysenck, 1959) and in particular, leads to psychomotor and intellectual errors, and disturbances of concentration and memory. At the other extreme, an absence of appropriate fear can foster dangerously careless behaviour. In many circumstances, moderate levels of fear seem to be adaptively valuable in the way proposed by Lazarus and others.

Examples drawn from military combat illustrate the value of appropriate fear; so do the observations made on surgical patients. Some additional instances of functional fear are seen in the use of seat belts, hygienic precautions, preparation for examinations, cessation of cigarette smoking and so on. Each of these last four examples has in fact been the subject of research and, in all cases, the adaptive behaviour was stimulated by the use of moderately fear-provoking communications. It appears, however, that communications which evoke high levels of fear are usually counter productive. Along similar lines, moderately fear-provoking messages can be counter productive if addressed to people who are already highly fearful or generally neurotic.

In an extensive study of American soldiers, Smith (1949) reported that inexperienced troops displayed little fear and carelessly disregarded safety measures. After exposure to combat, they became more vigilant, began to express fear and also made fewer careless errors. Smith's account implied that there was a causal sequence: calm and careless → combat → vigilance and fear → fewer errors.

In an interesting study on patients undergoing major surgery, Janis (1971) divided the patients into three groups based on the degree of fear which they expressed prior to undergoing the operation. The highly anxious patients continued to display considerable fear after the operation and also suffered a great deal of pain and discomfort. The moderately fearful patients coped better and showed little fear after operation and less pain. The unexpected finding was that those patients who were apparently fearless suffered an excessive amount of post-operative discomfort and pain and also displayed significantly more anger and resentment. Janis concluded that 'a moderate amount of anticipatory fear about realistic threats is necessary for the development of effective inner defences for coping with subsequent danger and deprivation.'

Supporting evidence for this view is provided by research into the immunising effects of warning people to expect stress. In a series of experiments Lazarus and his co-workers have shown that giving their subjects preparatory information significantly reduced the emotional distress produced by exposure to a stressful motion film. They have also demonstrated in a variety of studies that preparation involving certain types of mental rehearsal can also reduce the effects of stressful experiences, including fear. Egbert (1964) and others, tested the value of providing a large group of surgical patients with preparatory explanations about the expected type and duration of post-operative pain and related information, plus reassurance. Roughly half of the patients were given this extra preparation and the other half were given the conventional minimum of information. The fully prepared patients recovered more quickly and with less pain and discomfort.

In the light of a good deal of suggestive data, both Janis and Lazarus are confident that the mental rehearsal which often follows the arousal of fear can play a valuable role in helping to cope with real dangers and difficulties. If novel and sudden stimuli are both to be included in the list of stimulus qualities which are potentially fear-providing then we can account for at least a part of the effect of rehearsal – it acts to reduce both novelty and surprise. More generally, the effects of rehearsal can be incorporated into the model of a balance between habituation and sensitization to fear-evoking stimulation (chapter 9).

In general terms, the biological value of anticipatory fears is self-evident. It may be worth bearing in mind, however, that the relation between fear arousal and vigilance is of central interest. As we have seen, there is evidence that the emergence of anticipatory fear, by enhancing vigilance, may improve the chances of survival of combat soldiers. The biological value of fear is made most apparent by considering the likely fate of a totally fearless animal or, for that matter, a fearless person.

Who needs it?

So, despite its unpleasantness, fear is not always undesirable. We have also to consider those circumstances in which fear is thrilling and sought or simply tolerated while working for some other goal. Examples of striving for fear range from the childhood joys of hide-and-seek games, through the rides offered in fun fairs, up to motor racing. Although we do not have a satisfactory explanation of fear-seeking behaviour, the personality theory constructed by Eysenck is of some assistance.

According to Eysenck (1965, 1967, 1972) people can be described along at least two major dimensions of personality: extraversion–introversion and neuroticism. People can be plotted on these dimensions which range from one extreme to the other, passing through a middle area where people are neither fully the one personality type nor the other. Most people of course fall into the middle area. At the extremes, one may talk about the typical extravert and typical introvert.

It can be deduced from the theory that it is the extravert who is far more likely to engage in fear-seeking behaviour.

In a technical sense, the extraverted person is generally in a state of under-stimulation and hence engages in an active search for external sources of stimulation, including those of a fearful kind. Eysenck has provided a capsule description of the extremes found at either end of his extraversion – introversion dimension:

> The typical extravert is sociable, likes parties, has many friends, needs to have people to talk to and does not like reading or studying by himself. He craves excitement, takes chances, often sticks his neck out, acts on the spur of the moment, and is generally an impulsive individual . . . (Eysenck, 1965, p. 59).

On the other hand the typical introvert is

> a quiet, retiring sort of person, introspective, fond of books rather than people; he is reserved and distant except with intimate friends . . . tends to plan ahead and distrust the impulse of the moment. He does not like excitement, takes matters of everyday life with proper seriousness and likes a well-ordered mode of life . . . (Eysenck, 1965, p. 60).

After a complex chain of reasoning which need not be gone into here, Eysenck concluded that introverts characteristically are in a state of high internal stimulation whereas extraverts characteristically are in a state of low internal stimulation. He goes on to say that

> we can extend this whole notion by postulating that the extravert would be affected by what is sometimes called 'stimulus hunger', i.e. a desire for strong sensory stimulation – a desire which would be very much less marked in the introvert. Again, we can make certain testable deductions. We would expect extraverts for instance, to be fond of loud noise, jazz and bright colours; we would expect them to be keen on alcohol and other drugs, to smoke more cigarettes and to indulge in more fornication and in other types of sexual activity. There is a good deal of evidence that this is indeed so . . . the very sociability which is so characteristic a part of the extravert picture is possibly related to this stimulus hunger; most of our stimulation, after all, derives from concourse with other people and the well-known tendency of the introvert to settle down all by himself with a good book is certainly not conducive to providing the 'arousal jag' the extravert needs so badly, (Eysenck, 1965, pp. 84–85).

This concept of Eysenck's has considerable appeal on the grounds of its coherence, scope, neatness and ready applicability in everyday life. Applied to fear-seeking behaviour, it would enable us to make a large number of testable deductions of considerable interest – e.g. which people will seek and which one's avoid fear jags.

Another possibility, by no means incompatible with the first, is that deliberate self-exposure to fearful situations is prompted and repeated because of the enormous relief and satisfaction experienced after the event. Despite its whimsical aspects (e.g. wearing tight shoes in order to enjoy the relief and pleasure of taking them off), the idea is not entirely fanciful.

In order to account for some puzzling experimental findings, Gray (1971) argued that behaviour leading to the avoidance of fear is strengthened by the sight of safety signals. His argument is supported by numerous studies in which the power of safety signals is clearly demonstrated. Extrapolating to human behaviour, can it be that people endure acute fear in order to enjoy a terminal surge of relief? Is the immense relief of completing the course a sufficient motive to attract people to roller coasters? Possibly – but the owner of this weak stomach finds this perversity difficult to comprehend.

To conclude, the apparent paradox of people seeking fearful experiences may be seen as an attempt to obtain intense, external stimulation. Attempts of this type will commonly be made by highly extroverted people and assiduously avoided by prize introverts.

Appendix
Some Notes on Physiological Aspects of Fear

Are gut reactions *gut* reactions? We know from several sources (e.g. combat soldiers, psychiatric patients and some remarkable direct observations of a patient with a partially exposed stomach) that the stomach is involved in strong emotional experiences. Partly because research into the subject does not lend itself to elegant or easy experimental study, and partly because of a belief that gut reactions are gross indicators, comparatively little is known about them. We are however in a position to know that fear interrupts gastric activity. Cardiac responses, easy to record but tricky to interpret, are better understood. With some exceptions, heart rate appears to accelerate during fear. Clinically, one can observe the heart rate of phobic patients double from 70 to 140 beats per minute within seconds of their approaching a fear-provoking stimulus or situation. It comes as no surprise, then, to learn that one of the most prominent subjective experiences reported by fearful subjects or patients is that of palpitations. Measurements of skin conductance have featured largely in research into fear and other emotions, but it must be admitted that the return from most of this research has been meagre. Early hopes that the electrical activity of the skin might provide the longed-for thermometer of internal emotional states have not been fulfilled, despite useful advances in the technology of recording and quantification. The emotional significance of electrical activity in the skin appears, perhaps regrettably, to be limited.

It is fair to say that the poor return from research on electrical activity of the skin reflects what has been a general disappointment over the contribution made by psychophysiology to an understanding of emotional states and experiences. With exceptions, such as the distinction between fear and anger, psychologists have had little success in identifying psychophysiological patterns which are characteristic of specific emotional experiences. Instead it has been found that on the whole, psychophysiological reactions which accompany subjective emotional experiences are diffuse, non-specific and imperfectly correlated one with the other. The levels of psychophysiological reactivity range from intense excitement along a continuum to quiescence and none of the points along this scale is peculiar to, or indicative of, any specific emotional experience. Whether this lack of psychophysiological subtlety reflects our true constitution or the extent of our present ignorance, remains to be seen (Greenfield and Sternbach, 1972).

As far as fear is concerned, the experience and expression of this emotion is closely associated with the activity of the sympathetic branch of the autonomic nervous system. The 'opposite' state of calmness is associated with parasympathetic nervous activity. So, for example, cardiac acceleration, pupil dilation, increased skin conductance, gastric inhibition – all associated with fear – are mediated by the sympathetic nervous system. On the contrary, low and regular cardiac activity, high skin resistance, pupil constriction and gastric activity are all parasympathetic functions.

As already noted, it should not be concluded that sympathetic activity is necessarily indicative of fear. There is more than one pattern of sympathetic responding. So, for example, despite some common attributes (e.g. increased facial temperature), the patterns associated with fear and anger differ in respect of the cardiac element – the pulse rate is usually decreased in anger but rarely so in fear.

A prodigious amount of research on animals, supplemented by clinical observations of patients, has yielded considerable amounts of information about the emotional consequences of interventions, temporary or permanent, in the functioning of the central nervous system (see Grossman, 1967; Morgan, 1965). It is however proving to be exceedingly difficult to link and interpret the data in a coherent model of brain function (see Gray's recent stimulating interpretation). For convenience sake, the CNS is often conceived of having three major areas: the brain stem, mid-brain and cortex.

Stimulation of the brain stem produces fragmentary, isolated emotional reactions. The stimuli which provoke these primitive reactions are limited, unchanging and direct, while the reactions themselves are predictable, massive and short-lived. As one moves up the scale from the brain-stem through the mid-brain to the cortex, the reactions become better co-ordinated, directed and controlled. At the mid-brain level, the fragmentary reactions are ordered into a composite pattern. Both sympathetic and parasympathetic functions are integrated here, with the hypothalamus playing an important part in the regulation of emotional behaviour, including fear. It is generally assumed that this regulatory function is supplemented and partly controlled by the cortex which is responsible for the experience of emotion. Direct stimulation of the hypothalamus is, however, capable of producing coordinated and directed emotional reactions; fearful responses are most easily provoked by stimulation of the anterior sections and quiescence by stimulating the posterior sections. Theorists such as Gellhorn (1964) emphasize the reciprocal nature of the balance between the different areas, and his views have been quoted in support of Wolpe's (1958) theory of psychotherapy based on the reciprocal inhibition of fear/anxiety by relaxation or other responses incompatible with fear.

Research into the emotional functions of the cortex is continuing apace, and here I will mention only two general observations. Firstly, certain areas of the brain exert a controlling and restraining influence on the functioning of the lower centres. So, for example, damage to the frontal lobes can result in grossly disinhibited asocial behaviour. Secondly, the cortex plays a vital role in interpreting the stimuli which impinge on us. We have some fascinating examples of how stimuli (even when applied directly to specific, small areas of the brain) may, in certain social circumstances, produce one or other emotional reaction. For instance, direct stimulation of the monkey's brain may produce aggression in the presence of a submissive peer but little or no reaction in the presence of a dominant one (Delgado, 1969). Findings of this type provide a link with Schachter's writings (p. 35) on the importance of cognitive appraisal in the interpretation and experience of emotion, including fear.

Damage to the CNS can of course have serious emotional consequences, direct and indirect. Direct damage to certain areas may diminish a person's emotional responsiveness (e.g. patients who suffer spinal cord injuries or undergo surgical operations on the frontal lobes generally experience lessened fear reactions), while damage to other areas may lead to increased emotional irritability, including heightened fearfulness.

References

ABRAHAM, K. (1927), *Selected Papers*, Hogarth Press.

BANDURA, A. (1969), *Principles of Behavior Modification*, Holt, Rinehart & Winston.

BANDURA, A., BLANCHARD, E., and RITTER, B. (1969), 'The relative efficacy of desensitization and modelling approaches for inducing behavioural, affective and attitudinal changes', *J. pers. soc. Psychol.*, 13, pp. 173–99.

BEECH, R. (1968), *Changing Man's Behaviour*, Penguin.

BIANCHI, G. (1971), 'Origins of disease phobia', *Austral. J. Psychiat.* 5, pp. 241–57.

BROADHURST, P. (1960), 'Abnormal animal behaviour', in H. J. Eysenck (ed.), *Handbook of Abnormal Psychology*, Pitman.

CANNON, W. B. (1932), *Wisdom of the Body*, Norton.

COLLETT, L., and LESTER, D. (1969) 'The fear of death and the fear of dying', *J. Psychol.* 72, pp. 179–81.

DARWIN, C. (1872), *The Expression of the Emotions*, Murray.

DELGADO, J. M. (1969), *Physical Control of the Mind*, Harper & Row.

EGBERT, L. (1964), 'Reduction of post-operative pain', *New England J. Medicine*, 270, pp. 825–7.

EKMAN, P., FRIESEN, W., and ELLSWORTH, P. (1972), *Emotion in the Human Face*, Pergamon.

ENGLISH, H. (1929), 'Three cases of "conditioned fear response"', *J. abnorm. soc. Psychol.*, 34, pp. 221–5.

EPSTEIN, S., and FENZ, W. (1965), 'Steepness of approach and avoidance gradients in humans as a function of experience', *J. exp. Psychol.*, 70, pp. 1–12.

EPSTEIN, S. (1967). 'Towards a unified theory of anxiety', in B. Maher (ed.), *Progress in Experimental Personality Research*, Academic Press, New York.

EYSENCK, H. J. (ed.) (1960), *The Handbook of Abnormal Psychology*, Pitman.

EYSENCK, H. J. (1965), *Fact and Fiction in Psychology*, Penguin.

EYSENCK, H. J. (1967), *The Biological Basis of Personality*, Thomas, Springfield.

EYSENCK, H. J. (1972), *Psychology is About People*, Allen Lane.

EYSENCK, H. J., and RACHMAN, S. (1965), *The Causes and Cures of Neurosis*, Routledge & Kegan Paul.

FENZ, W. D. (1964), 'Conflict and stress', *Psychol. Mongr.* 78, no. 585.

FENZ, W. D., and EPSTEIN, S. (1967), 'Gradients of physiological arousal in parachutists', *psychosom. Med.*, 29, pp. 33–51.

FREUD, S. (1905 ed.) 'The analysis of a phobia in a 5-year-old boy', *Collected Papers, vol.* 3. Hogarth Press.

GELLHORN, E. (1964), 'Motion and emotion', *Psychol. Rev.* vol. 71.

GILLESPIE, R. D. (1945) 'War neuroses after psychological trauma', *Br. med. J.*, 1, p. 653.

GLOVER, E. (1956), *On the Early Development of Mind*, International Universities Press.

GOORNEY, A. B., and O'CONNOR, P. J. (1971), 'Anxiety associated with flying', *Br. J. Psychiat.*, 119, pp. 159–66.

GRAY, J. A. (1971), *The Psychology of Fear and Stress*, Weidenfeld & Nicholson.

GREENFIELD, W., and STERNBACH, R. (1972), *Handbook of Psychophysiology*, Holt, Rinehart & Winston.

GRIFFITHS, D., and JOY, M. (1971), 'The prediction of phobic behaviour', *Behav. Res. Ther.*, 9, pp. 109–18.

GRINKER, R., and SPIEGEL, J. (1945), *Men Under Stress*, Churchill.

GROSSMAN, S. P. (1967), *A Textbook of Physiological Psychology*, Wiley.

GROVES, P., and THOMPSON, R. (1970), 'Habituation: A dual-process theory', *Psychol. Rev.*, 77, pp. 419–50.

HAGMAN, G. (1932), 'A study of fear in pre-school children', *J. Exp. Psychol.*, 1, pp, 110–30.

HAMBURG, D. (ed.) (1967), *American Psychoanalytic Association*, report of an *ad hoc* committee, New York.

HOLMES, F. (1935), 'An experimental study of fears', *Child Devel. Mongr.*, no. 20.

HINTON, J. (1967), *Dying*, Penguin.

JAMES, W. (1890), *Principles of Psychology*, Holt, Rinehart & Winston.

JANIS, I. (1971), *Stress and Frustration*, Harcourt Brace & World, New York.

JERSILD, A., and HOLMES, F. (1935), 'Children's fears', *Child Devel. Mongr.*, no. 20.

JONES, E. (1955), *Sigmund Freud: Life and Work*, vol. 2, Hogarth Press.

JONES, M. C. (1924), 'A laboratory study of fear', *Pedagog. Sem.*, 31, pp. 308–15.

LADER, M., and MARKS, I. (1971), *Clinical Anxiety*, Heinemann Medical.

LADER, M., and MATHEWS, A. (1968), 'A physiological model of phobic anxiety and desensitization', *Behav. Res. Ther.*, 6, pp. 411–18.

LADER, M., and WING, L. (1966), *Physiological Measures, Sedative Drugs and Morbid Anxiety*, O U P.

LANDIS, C. (1924), 'Studies of emotional reactions', *J. comp. Psychol.*, 4, pp. 447–509.

LANDIS, C. (1929), 'The interpretation of facial expression in emotion', *J. genet. Psychol.*, 2, pp. 59–72.

LANG, P. (1970), 'Stimulus control, response control and desensitization of fear', in D. Levis (ed.), *Learning Approaches to Therapeutic Behaviour Change*, Aldine Press, Chicago.

LANG, P., and LAZOVIK, D. (1963), 'The experimental desensitization of a phobia', *J. abnorm. soc. Psychol.*, 66, pp. 519–28.

LANG, P., LAZOVIK, D. and REYNOLDS, C. (1966), 'Desensitization, suggestibility and pseudotherapy', *J. abnorm. soc. Psychol.*, 70, pp. 395–405.

LANG, P., MELAMED, B., and HART, J. (1970), 'A psychophysiological analysis of fear modification using an automated desensitization technique', *J. abnorm. Psychol.*, 76, pp. 220–34.

LAUTCH, H. (1971), 'Dental phobia', *Brit. J. Psychiat.*, 119, pp. 151–8,

LAWLISS, G. F. (1971), 'Response styles of a patient population on the fear survey schedule', *Behav. Res. Ther.*, 9, pp. 95–102.

LAZARUS, R. S. (1966), *Psychological Stress and the Coping Process*, McGraw-Hill.

LESTER, D. (1967), 'Experimental and correlational studies of the fear of death', *Psychol. Bull.*, 67, pp. 27–36.

MACKWORTH, J. F. (1969), *Vigilance and Habituation*, Penguin.

MARKS, I. M. (1969), *Fears and Phobias*, Heinemann.

MARKS, I. M. (1970), 'The origin of phobic states', *Amer. J. Psychother.*, 34, pp. 652–76.

MARKS, I. M., and GELDER, M. (1966), 'A controlled retrospective study of behaviour therapy in phobic patients', *Br. J. Psychiat.*, 111, pp. 561–73.

MARKS, I. M., and HERST, E. R. (1970), 'A survey of 1200 agoraphobics in Britain', *soc. Psychiat.*, 5, pp. 16–24.

MATHEWS, A. M. (1971), 'Psychophysiological approaches to the investigation of desensitization', *Psychol. Bull.*, 76, pp. 73–83.

MAY, R. (1950), *The Meaning of Anxiety*, Ronald Press, New York

MEYER, V., and CHESSER, E. (1970), *Behaviour Therapy and Clinical Psychiatry*, Penguin.

MILLER, N. E. (1969), 'Learning of visceral and glandular responses', *Science*, 163, p. 434.

MORGAN, C. T. (1965), *Physiological Psychology*, McGraw-Hill.

MOWRER, O. H. (1939), 'Stimulus response theory of anxiety', *Psychol. Rev.*, 46, pp. 553–65.

NEWMAN, L., and STOLLER, R. (1969), 'Spider symbolism and bisexuality', *J. Amer. Psychoanalytic Assn*, 17, pp. 862–72.

PAUL, G. (1966), *Insight versus Desensitization in Psychotherapy*, Stanford University Press.

RACHMAN, S. (1967), 'Systematic desensitization', *Psychol. Bull.*, 67, pp. 93–103.

RACHMAN, S. (1968), *Phobias: Their Nature and Control*, Thomas, Springfield.

RACHMAN, S. (1971), *The Effects of Psychotherapy*, Pergamon.

RACHMAN, S. (1972), 'Therapeutic modelling', *Behav. Ther.*, 3, pp. 379–97.

RACHMAN, S., and TEASDALE, J. (1969), *Aversion Therapy and the Behaviour Disorders*, Routledge & Kegan Paul.

RUTTER, M., TIZARD, J., and WHITMORE, S. (1970), *Education, Health and Behaviour*, Longman.

SACKETT, G. (1966), 'Monkeys reared in isolation with pictures as visual input', *Science*, 154, pp. 1468–72.

SCHACHTER, S., and SINGER, J. (1962), 'Cognitive, social and physiological determinants of emotional state', *Psychol. Rev.* 69, pp. 379–99.

SHEPHERD, M., OPPENHEIM, B., and MITCHELL, S. (1971), *Childhood Behaviour and Mental Health*, University of London Press.

SHERMAN, M. (1927), 'The differentiation of emotional responses in infants', *J. comp. Psychol.* 7, pp. 265–84.

SKINNER, B. F. (1953), *Science and Human Behaviour*, Macmillan.

SLATER, E. (1939), 'Responses to a nursery school situation', *Soc. Res. Child Devel. Mongr.*, no. 4.

SMITH, M. B. (1949), 'Combat motivations among ground troops', in *The American Soldier*, S.A. Stouffer (ed.), University Press, Princeton, New Jersey.

SPERLING, M. (1971), 'Spider phobias and spider fantasies', *J. Amer. Psychoanalytic Assn*, 19, pp. 472–98.

STAMPFL, T. (1970), 'Implosive therapy', in D. Levis (ed.), *Learning Approaches to Therapeutic Behavior Change*, Aldine Press, Chicago.

VALENTINE, C. (1930), 'The innate causes of fear', *J. genet. Psychol.*, 37, pp. 394–419.

WATSON, J., and RAYNER, R. (1920), 'Conditioned emotional reactions', *J. exp. Psychol.*, 3, pp. 1–22.

WOLPE, J. (1958), *Psychotherapy by Reciprocal Inhibition*, Stanford University Press.

WOLPE, J., and LANG, P. (1964), 'A fear-survey schedule for use in behaviour therapy', *Behav. Res. Ther.*, 2, pp. 27–34.

WOLPE, J., and RACHMAN, S. (1960), 'Psychoanalytic evidence: the case of Little Hans', *J. nerv. ment. Dis.*, 131, pp. 135–45.

Index

Abraham, K. 94
Adaptive behaviour 100
Agoraphobia 53, 54, 55, 58, 85
Air-crews 58, 79, 81
Air-raids 83
American soldiers 100
Analogue research 17, 19, 65
Anger 30, 31, 35, 36, 38, 106
Animal
 fear of 51, 56
 fears 44
 phobia 53, 54, 56, 81
Anxiety 13, 51, 55, 56, 77
Apprehension 79
Approach behaviour 33, 67, 71
Arousal
 of fear 101
 internal 37
 jag 103
 low 37
 physiological 35, 36
Auditory stimulation 48, 49
Automated desensitization 19, 20
Autonomic coward 24
Avoidance
 actions 77
 behaviour 20, 33, 76
 of fear 104
 gaze 42
 test 17

Bandura, A. 69, 71, 91
Beech, R. 62
Behaviour
 adaptive 100
 approach 33, 67, 71
 avoidance 20, 33, 76
 coping 71, 100
 fear-seeking 102, 104
 therapy 15, 62, 74
Behavioural avoidance tests 17, 65
Behaviourism 14, 40
Bianchi, L. 58
Biological value 102
Bisexual genitalia 94, 99
Blanchard, E. 69, 82
Blind children 30
Borneo 30
Brain stem 107
Brave autonomic system 24
Broadhurst, P. 77

Canadian experiments 80
Cannon, W. 34
Cardiac responses 105
Categories of emotion 29
Chesser, E. 62, 68
Children 43, 44, 46, 72, 75, 78, 79, 83
 fears of 83
Chimpanzees 41
Chinese 30
Chungking 30
Clinical effects 68, 69
Clinical phenomena 54
Cognitive factors 35

Collett, L. 57
Combat 79
Combat soldiers 58, 77, 105
Components of facial expression 31
Conditioning 61, 77, 79, 81, 82
Conditioning theory 76, 81
Confinement 77
Cortex 107
Courage 23, 24

Darwin, C. 25, 26, 76
Deceptions 32
Deformed people 50
Delgado, J. 108
Demonstration 78
Denial 32
Dental phobia 77, 80
Depressant drugs 87, 88
Depression 55, 56
Desensitization 15, 65, 66, 67, 68, 73, 74, 89, 90, 92, 93
Desynchrony 19
Disgust 31
Dying 52, 57

Early childhood 51, 56
Egbert, L. 101
Eight month anxiety 42
Ekman, P. 27
Electrical aversion therapy 82
Electrical resistance of the skin 37
Emotions
  categories of 29
  facial expression of 26, 28
  recognition of 25
English, H. 78
Environmentalism 40
Epstein, S. 21, 22
Euphoria 35, 36
Examinations 50
Exhaustion 55
Experimental neuroses 77
Expression
  components of facial 31
  non-verbal 27, 30, 31
  'principles' of 25
Extraversion-introversion 59, 102
Extravert 59, 60, 61, 102, 103, 104
Eyes, expressive 31
Eysenck, H. J. 40, 59, 60, 61, 62, 63, 68, 76, 80, 85, 100, 102–104

Facial expression of emotions 26, 28
Factorial analysis 50
Faint 52
Fear 80
  anticipatory 85, 101
  appropriate 100
  arousal of 101
  avoidance of 104
  clusters of 50
  distribution of 81
  elicited 84
  excessive 100
  extreme levels of 21
  incubation of 80
  intangible 13, 44, 49
  latent 95, 96, 97
  manifest 93, 95, 97
  prediction of 22
  tangible 13, 44, 49, 56
Fear arousal 102
Fear drive 77, 85
Fearful models 72
Fear jag 104
Fearless
  animal 102

approach behaviour 32
person 102
Fear of
animals 44
bees 48, 63
blood 50
children 83
dark 41, 46
darkness 42, 44
death 51, 56, 57, 58
disease 56, 58
figures in authority 53
harm 51
horses 95, 96
lambs 81
public speaking 19
snakes 41, 50, 66, 69, 81, 92
spiders 46, 92, 93
strangers 41, 43
water 51
Fear-provoking communications 100
Fears
abnormal 52
acquired 14
acute 13, 50
age-related 41
animal 44
causes of 14
chronic 12, 13, 50
circumscribed 17, 46, 48, 89, 98
decline in 43, 44
diffuse 12, 13, 48, 50, 56
distribution of 81
episodic 50
existentialist 56
focal 13
innately determined 14, 40, 41, 83
neurotic 13
normal 52
overcoming or reducing 73
pathological 52, 74
persistent 46, 48, 52
sexual 53, 54, 99
social 43
unconscious 99
Fear-seeking behaviour 102, 104
Fear thermometer 17
Feed-back 73
Feed-back control 38
Female fearfulness 51
Fenz, W. 21, 22
Flooding 15, 68, 69, 73, 74, 89, 90, 91
Focal fears 13
Freud, S. 76, 94, 95, 96
Frontal lobes 107, 108

Gastric activity 105
Gaze avoidance 42
Gelder, M. 46
Gellhorn, E. 107
Generalization 77, 78, 83
General rate of habituation 89
Germs 50
Ghosts 43
Gillespie, R. 79
Glover, E. 94
Goodenough, W. 29
Goorney, A. 81
Gray, J. A. 11, 40, 41, 42, 43, 79, 84, 104, 107
Greenfield, W. 106
Griffiths, D. 22
Grinker, R. 58, 79, 80
Grossman, S. 106
Groves, P. 86, 87
Gut reaction 105

Habituation 14, 41, 43, 44, 59, 83, 86, 87, 88, 89, 90, 91, 102

Hagman, G. 83
Happiness 26, 29, 30–32, 35
Hart, J. 20, 23, 88
Heart disease 58
Heart rate 23, 37, 38, 105
Hebb, D. 40
Herst, E. 55
High sensitivity 61
Hinton, J. 57
Holmes, F. 44, 45
Hygienic precautions 100
Hypothalamus 35, 107

Imitation 69, 71
Immunising effects 101
Implosive therapy 69
Individual differences 59, 80
Infants 28
Inner functions 38
Intellectual errors 100
Intense fears 69, 79
Intense stimuli 42, 49, 84
Intensity factor 43, 77, 86
Internal arousal 37
Internal bodily states 33
Internal stimulation 103
Interpretive methods 67
Intrinsic differences, fear stimuli 82
Introspectionist 40
Introvert 59, 102–104
Inventories 50
Isolates 41

James, W. 33, 34, 35
Janis, I. 101
Jersild, A. 44
Jones, E. 94
Jones, M. C. 62–4, 71
Joy, M. 22
Joy 35

Kamikazis 58

Lack of stimulation 42
Lader, M. 89, 91
Landis, C. 27, 28
Lang, P. 20, 23, 50, 65, 66, 88, 89
Lautch, H. 80
Lawliss, G. 51
Law of effect 76
Lazarus, R. S. 100, 101
Leeds 30
Lester, D. 56, 57
Little Albert 62
Little Hans 94, 95
Loneliness 56
Low arousal 37

Mackworth, J. 84, 86, 87
Main components 12
Male fearfulness 51
Marks, I. 41, 42, 46, 54, 55, 56, 68, 79
Mathews, A. 23, 88
Maturation 41
Melamed, B. 20, 23, 88
Mental rehearsal 101
Meyer, V. 62, 68
Mid-brain 107
Military combat 100
Miller, N. 38, 40, 76
Mitchell, S. 44
Mobbing 41
Modelling 15, 71, 73, 75, 82, 91
Monkeys 41
Morgan, C. 106
Motivating properties 76, 77
Motor racing 102
Muscle relaxation 64
Muscular tension 23, 79

Neurotic disorders 15

Neuroticism 59, 60, 102
Neurotic, phobia 46
Neurotics 59, 61
Newman, L. 94
Noise 43, 44
Non-verbal expression of fear 27, 30, 31
Novel stimuli 42, 49, 84
Novelty 43, 77, 86
Novices 21
Nursery school 46
Nurture 40

Obsessions 55, 56
O'Connor, N. 81
Oedipus complex 96, 97
Oppenheim, B. 44
Order of change, fear indices 19
Outcome measures 20
Overcoming or reducing fears 73
Overprotected 46

Palpitation 79, 105
Panic 52, 53
Parachute jumpers 21, 36
Parasympathetic 107
Passive 30
Patients, phobic 105
Paul, G. 19
Pavlov, I. P. 76
Personality 48, 59, 67, 68, 98, 102
Peter, case of 62, 63
Phobias 52, 54, 56, 59, 60, 67
  animal 53, 54, 56, 81
  bee 63
  dental 77, 80
  disease 58
  mini- 17
  social 53–56
  sexual 53, 54
Phobic 53
  defence 93
  neurotic 46
  patients 105
  reactions 78
  subjects 36
Physiological arousal 35, 36
Physiological indices 20
Pittsburgh University 65
Pleasantness 30, 31
Predators 43
Premonitory signs 38
Prepotent fear stimuli 84
Principles of emotional expression 25
Prolonged exposure 68, 72, 80, 91
Pseudo-therapy 66
Psychiatric disorder 48
Psychiatric patients 50, 51
Psychoanalysis 15, 74, 92
'Psychoanalytic' fears 98
  theories 32, 92
Psychodynamic theories 13, 69
Psychological defence 93
  disorders 62
Psychometric ratings 65
Psychophysiological recordings 18
  indices 67
  patterns 106
Psychotherapy 15, 74, 107
Public speaking 50
Punishment 61

Rabbits 62
Rachman, S. 62–9, 74–6, 81–5, 91, 96
RAF crews 81
Rayner, R. 62, 78

Reactions
'as if' 34
bodily 35, 36, 52
defence 97
inner 37
phobic 78
Readiness to respond 86
Reciprocal inhibition 89, 107
Recognition of emotions 27
Reinforcement theory 91
Relaxation 66, 67, 74, 90
Repetition 77
Repression 13
Reward 61
Reynolds, C. 66
Ritter, B. 69
Rutter, M. 46

Sackett, G. 41
Sadness 30–32
Safety measures 100
Safety signals 104
Schachter, S. 35–7, 108
Scoline 80
Self-reports 20
Sensitivity 86
Sensitization 14, 43, 86, 87, 102
Sensitizing 87
Separation anxiety 42
Sex difference 51
Sex symbolism 92
Sexual identification 92
Sexual life 98
Sexual problems 56, 97
Sharp objects 50
Shepherd, M. 44
Sherman, M. 27, 28
Siegel, J. 58, 79, 80
Singer, J. 35
Skin conductance 105
Skinner, B. F. 38, 91
Slater, E. 46, 47
Smith, M. B. 100
Social interaction 42, 43
Social transmission of snake fears 82
Special evolutionary dangers 42
Specific precipitants 81
Sperling, M. 92–4
Spider
fear of 46, 92, 93
symbol 93
Spinal cord injuries 108
Spontaneous fear reduction 72
Stampfl, T. 68
Steering functions 35
Sternbach, R. 106
Stimulus
attributes 42
configurations 79
hunger 103
intense 42, 49, 84
novel 42, 49, 84
sudden 42, 49, 84
Stoller, R. 94
Subjective feelings 35
Subjective reports 11
Suddenness, factor of 42, 86
Suffocating 53
Suicide 58
Surgical patients 101
Surprise 25, 30, 31
Symbolism 99
Sympathetic activity 106, 107
Systematic desensitization 64

Teasdale, J. 82
Tension 55
Terminal surge of relief 104
Terror 25, 26
Tests, behavioural avoidance 17, 65
Therapeutic modelling 69

Therapy
  behaviour 15, 62, 74
  electrical aversion 82
  implosive 69
  psycho- 15, 74, 107
The Open Door 55
Theories
  conditioning 76
  psychoanalytic 32, 92
  psychodynamic 13
  reinforcement 91
Thompson, R. 86, 87
Timid 46, 51
Traumatic
  conditioning 80
  dental experience 80
  stimulation 79

Unadaptive 52
Under-stimulation 103
Universal forms of emotion 26, 30

Valentine, C. 78
Veterans 21
Vicarious learning 82, 91
Vicarious transmission 83
Vigilance 100, 101, 102
Visual cliff 21

Watson, J. B. 62, 76, 78
Wing, J. 88, 90
Wolpe, J. 50, 62–5, 76–8, 89–91, 96, 107

Introducing Psychology

An Experimental Approach

D. S. Wright, Ann Taylor,
D. Roy Danes, W. Sluckin, S. G. M. Lee and J. T. Reason

Introducing Psychology was specially commissioned by Penguin Education from some of the staff of the Department of Psychology at the University of Leicester; their collaboration provides a wide range of specialist views within the coherence of a common framework and a consistent style.

After an introductory Part One on the scope of the book and on observational and experimental method in psychology ('the strongest unifying bond of the present book'), Part Two relates heredity, maturation and physiology to behaviour. A discussion of perceptual processes is followed by chapters on the effects of early experience, learning processes, the development of skills, and remembering. This last chapter leads on to the discussion of symbolic processes, which is the concern of the chapters on language and thinking in Part Four. In Part Five the authors explore methods of measuring individual differences, and discuss the notions of intelligence, personality and normality. In Part Six a chapter on some mechanisms of social influence describes recent work, in which basic principles of learning have been extended to the two-person situation. This is followed by a review of certain aspects of socialization and the book ends with a chapter on persuasive communications and the determining influence of group membership upon an individual's behaviour.

'It is a pleasure to note the clarity of exposition in the Leicester book, which amply demonstrates that serious writing does not have to be jargon-ridden in order to be scientific, nor colloquial in order to be readable . . . the Leicester book is heading for nomination as 'Best Buy' in the *Which?* sense. Quite apart from its positive merits, its price even for a paperback is amazingly low.'
British Journal of Psychology

The Pelican History of Psychology

Robert Thomson

The Pelican History of Psychology is probably, both in span and latitude, the most comprehensive history of the subject in print.

Too often other histories are anxiously concerned with philosophical concepts, confine themselves to the progress of basic experimental research and stop short at the 1920s. Robert Thomson, on the other hand, extends his scope outside the main stream of theory, deals with ideas which are specifically psychological, and brings his history far enough forward to discuss the trends which have developed since 1945. His outline of the birth of psychology in the early nineteenth century, of Darwin's impact, the achievements of the first generation of German, British, French, and American psychologists, and the major theories of Freud, Jung, and the Behaviourists, among others, is clear, logical, and authoritative: but his book extends beyond that.

The development of psychology in the years between 1918 and 1940 is traced by the author of *The Psychology of Thinking* in all its forms. Psychiatry, child psychology, industrial and social psychology, intelligence and personality testing are among the branches he discusses historically.

With its wide coverage and full bibliography, this introductory history will appeal to students of psychology particularly: but it also provides the general reader with a sound and simple outline of the growth of a science which, in little over a century, has developed from a fringe activity to a central and potent study.

Techniques of Persuasion

J. A. C. Brown

Attempts to change the opinions of others are as old as human speech, but in recent years we have come to fear that our thoughts and feelings are open to manipulation by new methods and hidden techniques. To the pressures of the 'admen' are added a whole battery of *hsi nao* (literally 'wash brain') techniques.

Here is a timely and much-needed survey of the whole area of persuasion. Dr Brown, the author of *Freud and the Post-Freudians*, ranges from political propaganda, religious conversion and commercial advertising, through a detailed appraisal of the intentions and effects of the mass media, to a cool look at case histories of indoctrination and confession.

But *Techniques of Persuasion* is more than a review of the phenomena of persuasion: it also contains a lucid analysis of the concept of personality itself. Only if we understand first the development of the central personality can we understand the importance of attempts to change it.

Intelligence and Personality
Their Assessment and Relationship

Alice Heim

Q. Which is the odd man out of the following words?

courage leaves measles steamer

A. Only *courage* has four vowels. Only *leave* has one syllable. Only *measles* is plural. But the correct answer is *steamer*... and you'll never guess why.

In this introductory study of intelligence and personality tests, Alice Heim, of the Cambridge Psychological Laboratory, frequently champions the frustrated 'Subjects' of capricious test questions.

Two main themes run through her critical description of intelligence, creativity and personality tests of various kinds (from the Allport-Vernon Study of Values to the Brook Reaction Test): first, that psychological phenomena (including dreams, imagery and feelings) do exist and are worth studying; and secondly, that in the 'oneness' of human nature, intelligence and personality are intimately linked and cannot truly be assessed in separate compartments. She attaches much of the blame for present dichotomies in psychology to the rigid and over-simplifying behaviour of behaviourists, with their unimaginative experiments on rats, cats and monkeys.

This is in places an angry book. But, with its lively comments on the role of heredity or the mediocrity of women, it entertainingly and clearly outlines the specialized field of testing in all its aspects.